Overcoming Anxiety

Self-Help Anxiety Relief

David Berndt, PhD

Clinical Psychologist

Other publications by David Berndt, PhD:

Western Psychological Services, Los Angeles:

Multiscore Depression Inventory

Multiscore Depression Inventory for Children

(with Charles Kaiser)

Author Friendly Publishing

Special Topics On Anxiety

(release date late October 2015)

Cooling Off: Turning Down the Heat on Anger

(May 2016)

Dedication

Dedicated to my patients, who have taught me a great deal more than I have taught them about how to use these techniques successfully. Thanks for your collaboration, courage and your ability to believe in and explore your own resources.

Become a charter member of Dr. Berndt's Psychology Knowledge Readers Group and get free information and excerpts from his books.

Introduction

As a clinical psychologist who works every day with clients to help them find ways to navigate their anxiety, I have had the privilege of teaching, developing, and refining, with the feedback and input of my clients, several useful anxiety management tools. Many of the techniques stand on the shoulders of my peers and mentors. In addition to providing a strategy for anxiety relief, several of the skills introduced in this book also are applicable to managing worries, panic, and dread.

Anxiety medication can sometimes be helpful as well, but medication interventions are not the focus in these pages. Indeed, anxiety medication, while effective in treating anxious feelings, serves as a support in much the way a leg brace can help hold an injured knee steady. The aim of psychotherapy, to continue this metaphor, is more akin to working on stretching and exercising leg muscles so that you can regain balance and walk normally again without external support. The strategies and exercises in *Overcoming Anxiety* have been very helpful when implemented by my clients, and these tools can help you to deal with anxiety if you adopt and modify some of the ideas.

Of course the support and feedback of a trusted therapist who can fine-tune these and other strategies is a good idea, and a good therapist can see your problems with a fresh set of eyes. A therapist brings the wisdom of practical experience helping people like you, and having one as an ally is nearly always better than going it alone, or relying solely on pills.

The first five chapters explore various techniques from which you can draw, and once you have understood and mastered them, I encourage you to combine, customize, or borrow from the various procedures so they become tailor-made for you, and your unique situation.

For those who want to gain a better grasp of anxiety as a disorder of the brain and body, I have followed these early chapters with some educational material in Chapter Six; if you need to know more about the biological and neurophysiological components of anxiety you might want to skip to those materials, where I discuss these aspects in a way that I hope is accessible. Each chapter can be read independently, however the information may be easier to understand when read in sequence.

The methods discussed in *Overcoming Anxiety* do not focus exclusively on cognitive behavioral therapies for anxiety. In that distinction, it differs from most of the modern books on anxiety, especially those in the self-help literature. Some useful cognitive techniques are discussed and relied upon throughout the book, especially in

Chapter Five, which is drawn, although with some creative license, from the cognitive approaches most commonly recommended to anxious patients, whether in the self-help or mental health literature.

The earlier chapters tend to explore tools drawn from a variety of therapeutic approaches. More than anything, the methods introduced in the first five chapters were selected because I wanted to share with you the approaches that my patients and I have found most helpful in the trenches.

Table of Contents

Chapter One
Managing Anxiety by Coming to Your Senses

I wanted to start off by teaching you a technique, sometimes known as the 54321 Technique, you can begin to use today. I learned a version of this initially from another psychologist, Yvonne Dolan (1991, 2000), who is one of the bright stars of the Solution Focused brief therapy approach. Perhaps because of her training under master therapist Milton Erickson, she learned the value of being especially creative and innovative. When I noticed early in my career that my skill set needed some bolstering, I sought training from Ms. Dolan, among others. She taught an earlier version of this technique in a seminar that

I attended on treatment approaches to Post Traumatic Stress Disorder.

The information she shared is presented in her 2000 book, *One Small Step, Moving Beyond Trauma and Therapy to a Life of Joy.* She indicated that the technique in its original version should be credited to Betty Erickson, the wife of hypnotherapist Milton Erickson (Erickson, Rossi, and Rossi 1977). This particular method, as it has evolved in the way I use it, is now one of my "go to" tools whenever I want to help my clients to feel more grounded. Yvonne Dolan originally taught me the approach as a tool for dealing with flashbacks, so it is a fairly strong remedy, but my patients and I have discovered that it can be useful with many types of emotional storms.

Ms. Dolan encouraged those of us who were in that PTSD training seminar to continue to develop what I will call the "54321 Technique," and to modify it. The 54321 moniker is probably the way it is most widely used. I have, over the years, had the privilege—with significant input from many of my clients—to change, improve upon, and modify some components of this procedure. I now use the tool clinically as I present it here, to teach my clients how to manage anxiety and other strong feelings.

Custom Designed

The way I am presenting this technique is easy to teach, and in order to present it to the reader I have similarly made it as accessible as possible, and in so doing, by necessity I am making it rather generic. I leave it up to you the reader to shape it, change it, and enrich it in ways that are tailored to your own unique needs and style. As you become more skilled at the basic procedure (and others presented in later chapters), you will find ways to improve the technique by making it more interesting to you, more simpatico, and thereby more powerful.

In its simplest form this 54321 skill can be quite helpful without any changes. However, by changing the technique and making it yours, you will more confidently rely on it for managing severe anxiety and for relief during other peak moments of stress. Combined with other strategies in the later chapters, you will get more adept at developing an emotionally intelligent skillset, from which you can pick and choose your best option for handling an emotional problem.

How and When the 54321 Technique Works

Before we start, I want to explain a bit about how the method works. This technique is a good way to learn to subdue or harness most emotions, like anxiety, anger, panic, or fear, when they become unmanageable. Once mastered, this skill has the potential to work well and simply when these emotions are creating havoc in your life.

This method will not completely rid you of your anxieties or fear, and it does not—and should not—entirely stop all worry or fretting. It will not solve all your pressing emotional problems. What it *can* do is shrink your troubling—and often overwhelming—feelings, so they can become smaller, more manageable, and less compelling.

You don't necessarily want to lose your ability to feel fear, or anxiety, because these feelings can be useful.

Let me explain why: anxiety is a signal to you that something may already be wrong, or is about to become a serious problem. It is like a yellow light at a traffic signal. It tells you "wait a second, something is up!" When you are afraid, you usually have a good idea about what it is causing the fear; but anxiety, while at least equally disturbing, can be harder to pin down. The extra uncertainty usually makes anxiety feel worse than any straightforward fear.

You don't necessarily want to get rid of the signal, you simply want to make it smaller instead of letting it grow out of proportion. Anxiety, when managed, can be a useful cue that you need to act. If a situation alarms or frightens you, you should probably find a way to fix the problem—to do something—and not necessarily freeze or run.

This is true with many such feeling signals. If you bend your leg too far in one direction, you feel pain, and the signal tells you to stop bending it. If you cut yourself, the pain signal alerts you to take care of the wound right away. But if the pain is *too big*, then it could drive you bonkers, or at least keep you awake.

So, too, with anxiety. Anxiety, fear, and worry definitely can have a place in our lives, warning us that something is amiss or needs your attention. However, these feelings create problems when they overwhelm us rather than alert us, and prevent us thereby from making the changes that are needed.

To go back to the traffic light metaphor, if you make use of the yellow light at the signal, then you change your speed—slow down or speed up—in order to avoid a collision. But if the yellow light was so bright and flashing that you wouldn't pay attention to the intersection, then the signal is not of much use. It might even cause you to crash, or sit there dazed in the middle of the crossroads until a semi takes you out.

When trying to control anxious feelings, the idea is to learn how to shrink, but not get rid of, that enormous feeling. The technique I am introducing in the current chapter teaches you to use your five senses to that effect. It "grounds" the strong feelings in your body, in much the same manner as an electrical ground releases the pent up electrical charge that it drains off.

The 54321 Technique, as I am teaching it, is

connected to, and makes good use of, three different approaches to managing feelings. *Distraction* is one component often used in anxiety management, and it is an important feature of this procedure. The *mindfulness* literature popularized by Jon Kabat-Zinn, (1991 and 2003) and more recently discussed by psychologists like Sears and his colleagues (2011), provides a body of knowledge that was also drawn upon in developing this technique, at least in its current sensory form. The third approach that is a central part of the 54321 method relies on some components of *self-hypnosis*. The self-hypnosis that is used here is easy to do, and easy to learn, just by mastering the technique presented in this chapter. Each of these three components will be briefly discussed.

Distraction as a Way to Manage Anxiety

Imagine a child you are responsible for is

throwing a temper tantrum. What can you, as an adult, do that can make the child stop howling? If your six-year-old nephew is along on your shopping trip, and he gets it in his head that he wants some extra candy or that chocolate-coated cereal, what can you do (besides give it to him)?

Distracting such a child is one approach that works fairly well. You can distract the nephew with a serious threat and a loud voice, or maybe with some tickling, or a bribe, but a more pleasant and effective way is to just get him thinking or talking about something else. If your niece is a fan of Disney, you can get her talking about the trip the family has planned for next week to Disneyland and whether she wants to see the parade. If your six-year-old nephew is into collecting coins, you can pull out a pocketful, and soon he will be raptly inspecting your change for a possible silver quarter or Indian head nickel. Whatever is most compelling to the child is what works best.

Adults do not have as many temper tantrums, but distraction works just as well with an adult version of these emotional storms, and you can use it on yourself. Indeed, many of the classic techniques of anxiety management utilize distraction to redirect anxiety. In the midst of your own severe anxiety you simply find a distraction that interests you, and then run with it.

The idea is straightforward: if you can find a way to distract yourself—or have someone else distract you—then that distraction takes your attention away from the anxiety. Of course distraction works best when you find the diversion sufficiently interesting, so that it can easily grab hold of your attention.

As in the tantrum example above, the distraction should be something that you like, are interested in, or that you find compelling for some other reason. It has to be at least as interesting—ideally more so—than the thing causing the emotional storm. If the child is not interested, he will go back to the tantrum, and if the adult cannot find an interesting diversion, then the anxiety will not recede.

The 54321 Technique, as I teach it, makes good use of the principal of distraction as a core component or feature and it teaches you compelling ways to distract yourself from your anxiety. Using the 54321 Technique, you can get really good at finding basic ways to distract yourself from your anxiety. Distraction, however, is only one of three features of the method I am introducing.

Mindfulness- Acceptance of the Present Moment

For the purposes of teaching the 54321 Technique, I will be asking you to get distracted by noticing your world around you, in the here and now, using three of your five senses.

While there are plenty of things you could think of that would capture the imagination, maybe even more completely than the real-time experience of your senses, we are all, when given the chance, typically more than a little interested in what we see, hear, feel, smell, and taste. I am, in introducing this technique, utilizing your ability to be aware of your five senses in an accepting and appreciative way. In part, I ask you to use your senses because they can be easy to access, and for me to use as a quick demonstration. It just so happens that this use of the senses, at least in this way, is resonant with another area of psychological scrutiny and practice: mindfulness.

Mindfulness research (e.g., Greenson, 2009; Hofmann et al. 2010) has shown that paying attention appreciatively or acceptingly to what your senses are experiencing in the moment can be a very powerful clinical tool for dealing with anxiety and a number of other emotional problems. Directing your awareness in this fashion, as part of a mindfulness exercise, is a proven way to bring your feelings under better control, decrease stress, or lift your sense of well-being. For the purposes of this chapter, I will not go into an in-depth discussion of mindfulness, but I will revisit mindfulness again briefly in Chapter Five when we discuss cognitive therapies.

However, I want to acknowledge that one of the reasons I currently teach my technique with an emphasis on the senses is my admiration for, and appreciation of, the mindfulness approach. The 54321 Technique utilizes some basic mindfulness principles, modified of course, to the task at hand.

In mindfulness, you are asked to bring your awareness to the here and now, purposefully, but without judgment. You are expected to have a curious and open-minded acceptance of everything that comes to your attention, returning to the present moment sensations should you drift into the past or future. To the extent that thoughts intrude, you simply note them with acceptance or curiosity, just as you notice your senses or bodily sensations.

Most people find that this kind of attention to their senses is compelling, but some people seem to be more adept at visualizing, while others are more comfortable with hearing and auditory phenomena. Still others are "touchy feely" and can't refrain from using and cultivating their sense of touch. Some clients can most easily get lost instead in the senses of smell or taste.

Take a second and remember what you did yesterday, after 7:00 p.m. When you searched your memory, just now, did you pay more attention to a visual image, or did you hear "words" or other sounds. Did you go straight to a recall of smells or tastes? How about touch?

Chances are good that the way you remembered last night is the way you usually process the world around you, and it is good to know what your favorite senses are—the ones you rely on the most or tend to favor.

These sensory styles were referred to as "representational systems" when they were introduced by Bandler and Grinder (1979) in Neuro-Linguistic Programming (NLP). If you have a preferred sensory modality, a favored sense or favored senses, then that sense will be more compelling if you are cultivating your sensory awareness.

Mindfulness often encourages you to get absorbed in all five of your senses, in the present moment, with an attitude of appreciation or acceptance. This practice has been shown to decrease stress, and your mind and emotions typically become more placid.

For the purposes of the 54321 Technique, I want you to choose three of your preferred senses. You are going to use this technique to learn to distract yourself by getting a little lost in the momentary experience of three of your favorite sensory modes. Betty Erickson also asked you to pick three senses, but in her original version, it was sight, sound, and touch. You can pick your favorite three.

Ericksonian Self-Hypnosis as Part of the 54321 Skill

In addition to distraction and mindfulness, the 54321 Technique utilizes self-hypnosis and most especially some principles from Ericksonian hypnosis (Rosen 1991). Furthermore, the original technique appears to have been developed by Betty Erickson as a technique she used for self-hypnosis.

You don't need to understand or know anything about self-hypnosis to use the 54321 Technique, but since it does make use of this phenomenon, a brief discussion of self-hypnosis is in order. If you want to skip this section, and get right to the technique later in this chapter, that is fine.

Self-hypnosis is something you already know how to do, although you may never have realized you were doing it. Have you ever been really absorbed in a movie—so much a part of the experience that you found yourself swept up in it? If so, you were at that moment, in something of a simple, self-induced trance. You were lost, as it were, in the movie.

I remember going to see Steven Spielberg's *Jurassic Park*, and when the Raptors bit through the ceiling, trying to devour the children running upstairs, I lifted my feet off the floor. Now, at some level I knew that I was in a movie theater, and that there were no dinosaurs underneath me, biting at my feet. Yet I was so "into" the movie, that I was not aware of the theater or popcorn; instead I was aware of the Raptors.

This kind of absorption is a key component of effective self-hypnosis, and you can make use of that kind of absorption in the 54321 Technique. I bet, if you think about it, you can find other times you have been completely focused on something.

Athletes recognize when they are "in the zone", because their performance is at its peak; everything else fades, and all that is left is the target or goal. Anybody who routinely dominates a sport likely uses self-hypnosis, although many successful athletes take it for granted, and are often unaware that they have mastered it, unless they seek out a sports psychologist to refine this skill.

Highway hypnosis is a term we use to describe what happens to you when you lose track of several exits while driving a long boring stretch of highway. What was going on? Where were you? Why, when this happens, do you not get a ticket, and how do you avoid getting into an accident?

These examples of everyday self-hypnosis should take away some of the mystery. In the

54321 Technique, you get absorbed in your senses, in much the same way Michael "Air" Jordan gets absorbed in the hoop when he is flying to the net, or LeBron James engineers a triple double on a good night. You don't cluck like a chicken, you focus.

In addition to absorption, 54321 has other built in aspects of hypnosis, and one of those is the idea of fractionation. Fractionation was popularized by Neuro-Linguistic Programming (NLP), but it likely originated with Milton Erickson (Erickson, Rossi, and Rossi 1977). A renowned hypnotherapist and psychiatrist (he also invented family therapy), Erickson perfected many of the more successful hypnosis techniques. While hypnotherapists might use various techniques to "deepen" a trance experience, Erickson noticed that going in and out of trance could really intensify the experience. The same principle applies to experiencing alternating deeper and shallower levels of absorption.

Erickson figured out that this was a useful method for deepening a hypnotic experience, and that method, in its various forms, is called fractionation.

I think it would be helpful at this point to provide an example. It is now standard fare for hypnosis to use imagery like descending a set of stairs, counting as you descend, in order to deepen a trance and to intensify the level of your absorption that can accompany that deepening. One such method is to use a "countdown" to guide an individual into a deeper level of relaxed absorption. You can, for example, simply count backwards from 10 (or any starting number), with each number signifying to yourself a deeper level of absorption.

If I am using such an approach to hypnotize a client I will ask that person to imagine some useful image that they enjoy—one that can also convey relaxation, serenity, comfort, focus, or whatever target state is desired. Some patients prefer counting down stairs, but it is not unusual for a client to pick something like clouds, trees, waves, or a sailboat tacking in the wind— whatever image most helps to move to a deeper level—a level that represents to the client a compelling depth of relaxation or focus.

However, as noted above, Erickson also discovered something else: fractionation. He noticed that moving in and out of the deepening absorption can make that trance more powerful and deeper. Instead of disrupting the trance-like absorption, because of the fluctuation the experience is magnified. For example, when you move up and down the steps unevenly the learning experience that results seems to facilitate going more deeply into the absorption.

It might be useful, in explaining fractionation, to give an example: when counting backwards from 10, instead of a straightforward linear descent, (for example 10, 9, 8, 7, etc.) it works better when the count instead goes unevenly up and down.

By illustration, in a regular self-hypnosis session, you might begin by saying to yourself something like:

Ten; Because I deserve a break, I am starting to really make myself relaxed and comfortable. By the time I reach one I will be totally absorbed in this relaxation and as comfortable as I would like to feel.

Nine; More relaxed and peaceful, as I breathe in and out fully, letting my worries and everything else fade away, and just noticing my slow, deep breathing, and how it feels.

Eight; Continuing the process, noticing the changes that have already started, and knowing that I am on my way to the level I want to have today.

Seven; That's right, already at a deeper level of comfort, while still alert and curious about what is happening…etc.

This deepening of your absorption/relaxation can be powerful when done in a way that is tailored to your own interests, preferences, and needs. If you pay attention to how you are feeling at each number, you can begin to get a sense of the difference between the depth of relaxation at the level eight, for example, and the greater depth at the level five.

Fractionation, however, makes the deepening process even more intensified.

What Erickson and others figured out was that if you don't count "10, 9, 8, 7 etc." but, instead, count down unevenly, like 10, 9, 8, 7, 8, 9, 8, 7, 6, 5, 6, 7, 6, 5, 4 etc., taking your time, of course, at each level, this "fractionation" makes the level of absorption/trance/relaxation that much deeper. With the uneven count, we seem to be able to learn to move in and out of different levels of trance more discernably. When, during a standard countdown, your inner critic wonders whether anything is really changing, that can detract and interfere. However, moving in and out (or up and down), seems to make the inner changes more tangible and real, and this facilitates the absorption.

The 54321 Technique makes use of both deepening and fractionation. You don't have to worry about understanding these ideas or even to bother about learning self-hypnosis in order to use the technique. We have built them into it. I just wanted to let you know some of its underpinning. You do not have to know specifically how to use fractionation; if you do it the way I am suggesting, then that whole process is included in technique.

You may, however, find it reassuring to know that the method that you are about to learn utilizes—despite its simplicity—some powerful internal processes, and uses them to good effect, to redirect your anxiety.

How to Use the 54321 Technique-The Basics

I am now going to introduce how the basic 54321 Technique is used. Later I will discuss how you can customize and enhance it, thereby making it all the more compelling. The basic version that I am about to show you is simple, and it can be used by anyone. That method works just fine, and this simple approach is the easiest way to teach it, and for you to learn to use it, when you initially practice the technique.

Because we all are interested in our senses, you can pick three of your favorite senses to distract you from the anxiety. Each time you do it can be a different three senses if you like. You are going to be very mindful of these three senses, appreciating them as you note the sensations in the here and now, and you are going to let them distract you.

The first couple of times you try this, it should be a practice/training session. It is not so easy that it should be tried without at least a few practice sessions to get out the kinks and begin to tweak it to fit your style. You probably should be alone, and in a comfortable, relatively unhurried place and time, ideally sitting up so you don't fall asleep, but lying down is fine if comfort dictates that. Once you get good at it (like any skill, practice makes it easier and stronger) you can do the basic 54321 Technique in the midst of chaos. No one will even know, although from the outside you might seem a little distracted. But for now, just get comfortable in a private place.

Pick any three of your senses, it doesn't matter which ones. First I am going to demonstrate it, and then you can do it.

This basic method goes like this: I am going to

pick three senses, in this instance seeing, hearing, and feeling. I will pay attention and notice appreciatively and fully, for a long moment, five things that I see, then five things that I hear, and then five things that I feel. Next, I will notice four more things that I see, then four things that I hear, and four things that I feel. Continuing on, I notice three things I see, and so on. By the time I reach level one, I am usually so comfortable, and so absorbed, that what was bothersome has largely faded away. I am, instead, in a place where I am aware, focused, and grounded, with a calmer mind and a more relaxed body.

As I attend to the things that I notice in the here and now, one sense at a time, I will spend a few moments with each item, lingering or even savoring the sensation before turning my attention to, and sensing the next thing. If I can't perceive anything right away I just wait a few more seconds, as something will come to my attention. While waiting, my senses are getting even sharper and more focused, with greater absorption.

As a demonstration I will type in an example now, and you can read along while I present it. (Note: if I were by myself, I would be just noticing these things not typing, and if I were teaching it to you in person, I would be saying it aloud rather than typing). If you were watching me demonstrate this in a clinical session, you would see that I am in no rush, and because I have enjoyed this process so many times, I notice my relaxation building right away, even as I am starting.

"I am sitting at the computer in my office, and I see
    the computer screen,
    and I see the wall behind it,
    now I see the printer,
    and the coffee cup,
    and the rug (5 things).

I hear

the xerox machine (it makes a lot of noises),

and the chair moves, squeaking as I fidget,

the click of the mouse,

and a car driving by, outside.

I hear someone just shut a door in the hallway.

I feel

the temperature here, it is not too hot, and not too cold,

and I feel the chair beneath me.

I feel my socks on my feet,

and I am aware that my left leg itches.

I feel my mouth is dry.

Now four more things I see. (You could notice the same ones, if you prefer, but I find that I need to change it up, to make it more compelling).

I see

the cream and coffee in the coffee cup,

and then the surface of the shoes that I am wearing.

I see the smudge that the desk made on the wall,

and I see the back of my own hands....

I hear

the air conditioning.

I hear my breathing, and notice that it has slowed...

I hear the hum of electricity in the fixtures.

I hear a bird singing outside.

I feel

my hair.... ;

I feel my belt.

I feel the air that I breathe in, in my nose, it is a different

temperature than the air I am breathing out.

I feel the absence of my wallet.

Three things now:

I see

    the weave of the carpet,

    the remote control,

    and the pattern of my socks....

I hear

    my heartbeat,

    and the noise of my tongue moving in my mouth,

    and someone talking several rooms over.

I feel

    one shoe feels tighter than the other,

    and my toenails, especially my little toe...

    I feel the inside of my head.

Two Things:

I see

    my knuckles,

    and what I just typed.

I hear

    A car pulling into the driveway;

my sigh just then…
I feel
my cheeks are relaxed,
and my eyes are dry.

I see the dusk starting to arrive out my window.
I hear myself swallow.
I feel my jaw, it's not quite as tense as it was."

If you lose track of the numbers, that is fine, it means it is already working. You do not have to make it all the way to level one. In fact I rarely need to go further than three because when I do it now it kicks in quickly. Certainly, by the time you get down to one thing you see, hear, or feel, you will likely be more relaxed and grounded in your body; if you are open to the process and not worried about getting it right, you can get really absorbed in the things to which you were paying attention.

When a distracting thought, sensation, or

feeling comes, make note of it, appreciatively, but do not spend much time or effort with it, simply direct your awareness back to the task at hand.

Simple, right? Well, it is supposed to be. You can practice this a couple of times, in a quiet place alone, and then, with a little more practice, you can get pretty good at it, and you will be able to do it with ease.

There are some key elements. You need three different categories of things to notice, so you can move in and out of them as you count down (this is how we get the fractionation boost discussed earlier). It is a whole lot easier to demonstrate this distinction (the need for three distinct categories) using three senses, which are clearly three different types of things. It can, however, be any three categories that are distinct and compelling. Until you have it mastered though, I recommend sticking to three of the five senses, one sense for each category. You can develop more advanced and interesting ways of doing 54321 later as you customize it.

The hardest part is remembering to use this technique. As I noted earlier, it is probably not a good idea to wait until you need it before you try it out. Instead, practice it first and get comfortable with it. Once you know the technique, and know that you can do it easily without effort or worry about whether you are doing it right, then it can be something you will be more likely to remember to use in a time of need. When anxiety runs amok, you will have the 54321 tool practiced and ready to use, with ease, as one of many grounding techniques that will give some anxiety relief.

Some Anecdotes to Illustrate Novel Uses

I had been sharing this technique with my clients for some time. Initially I used it exclusively for my clients with PTSD, who needed to manage their flashbacks, and later for others with severe anxiety. I was getting a lot of positive feedback from these clients. However, I had not tried it myself, except that first instance, in the seminar where I learned an earlier version of it from Ms. Dolan.

I really hadn't had a need for the technique myself, and I had not yet realized its potential for use in other kinds of problems. I felt a little self-conscious about not having worked with it myself, because usually I make it a practice to have several test runs before I ask others to try something new.

However, where I was working there was a pressing need for new and stronger grounding methods, and so I offered it right away to my trauma patients, in a manner that was much like the way it had been taught to me. I had not yet figured out ways to make it even better, and because I had not become truly familiar with it, I had not explored ways it could be applied, adapted, or customized.

One advantage of that for me was that by the time I got around to trying it, my clients had convinced me that it was a very useful and helpful tool.

My first time using it myself came in a surprising way. I tend to sleep pretty soundly, and typically I can fall to sleep without much trouble. Since I lived at the time in the foothills of the Smoky Mountains, listening to the babbling stream outside the window of my log cabin and a crackling fire in the fireplace made sleeping for me an easy and pleasant nightly routine.

One night, however, I could not get to sleep, even with all that lovely background noise. You likely have experienced what I was feeling: I was tossing and turning, well into the middle of the night, and so much so that I probably had tied all the sheets and blankets into knots.

The longer I persisted, trying unsuccessfully to fall asleep, the more I became aware of time passing, and of how tired I would be the next day. I didn't think of this restless keyed-up feeling as anxiety at the time, but it probably was. I certainly did not have any particular worries, but there was an intrusive physical tension and restlessness that kept me in perpetual motion at 2:30 a.m.

I started to get up, to get myself a drink of bourbon. This is what my parents used to call a "nightcap." I guess I had learned from them that liquor was an effective way of knocking yourself out in the middle of the night. So I was ready to try it—for the first time—as a treatment for my temporary insomnia.

It was then that I remembered the 54321 method. Maybe it could help. Five things I see (the logs in the log cabin, the embers of the fire in the fireplace, etc.) Five things I hear (the babbling brook of course, the cracking embers in the fireplace, and the owl hooting, etc.). And the five things I smelled...

The 54321 Technique is not really a technique for treating insomnia, or even to make you sleepy or tired. There are certainly more specialized methods I know and use more regularly to handle insomnia. But the 54321 Technique puts you in a neutral place, and it grounds you. Neutral worked just fine for me that night, and so I went right off to sleep.

I soon began to work on the technique more flexibly and found it was useful for many situations in which clients needed to tame big feelings. At the same time, my patients also taught me about new applications that they discovered, and changes they made that made it work better for them. It was a truly collaborative project. I would introduce the technique, or a modification to 54321, and I benefitted from feedback on what worked. The innovative things they did that helped make it work for them, or the new uses they found, were then added to my arsenal.

On one occasion, not long after I began to really experiment with the 54321 Technique, I stumbled into another way to use it. I had a long (nearly three hour) drive from my log cabin to the airport that I used for most of my travel. As usual, I stopped for coffee and a bite to eat on the way, and I ordered a big bowl of chili, since the weather was cold and snowy. By the time I was on the 285 bypass approaching Hartsfield International Airport in Atlanta, I was feeling my chest tighten, and my heart was starting to beat rapidly. At first I thought the traffic, which can be daunting, somehow had me spooked. After all, I had become used to driving on rural roads, and I thought maybe I had just forgotten what it was like to drive as part of the hustle and bustle of expressways. However, while traffic eventually thinned, the sensations continued to increase. By the time I pulled into the road leading to the airport, I began to wonder if I was afraid my plane would crash, or maybe I was I having a panic attack.

Now *I do not* have panic attacks, and I am definitely *not afraid* of flying; I do it all the time. So, I started thinking: this might be a real heart attack. By now, my heart was beating really fast. Or maybe I somehow knew about the fate of the particular plane that I was taking? My mind was spinning and I felt certain I was going to go crazy if couldn't get more oxygen. It felt like an elephant sitting on my chest. Well, if it was a heart attack, I would have to get some help pretty fast. No, I thought, this *had* to be what a panic attack feels like.

I usually park in the long term parking (yes, I am a cheapskate) but something was up, that much I knew. So I parked in the most expensive space, one right next to the terminal. By the time I was past the ticket counter and through the security search, it felt worse than I could have imagined; I was sure everybody knew something was up, and I started looking out of the corner of my eye for the closest medic. I couldn't breathe, or think, and I thought I was suffocating.

At the D concourse, I got in line at a Starbucks™-type of kiosk and realized I needed to do something, so why not start with what was there at hand.

"OK," I said to myself, "I can see five different ways they serve coffee (savoring each as I noticed them)…five things I can taste (from among the scones and other baked treats)…five things I smell…." Before I got to the front of the line, my chest was no longer tight, my breathing and heart rate had slowed, and I was left with only a real sensation that I could now, fortunately, explain.

It turned out that I was not having a heart attack, or foretelling a plane crash. However, I also knew now to not buy the coffee. I bought a scone and proceeded to the gift shop and bought the needed remedy. Not the pharmacy, no you read it correctly, the gift shop.

What I realized by the time I got to the front

of the line was that chili was the culprit. The bowl I had eaten on an empty stomach early in the drive to the airport had sent my body and mind into panic mode. The chili was giving me a little heartburn or acid reflux. I had blown it way out of proportion, of course, and somehow mistook that for something scary. This "panic attack" was easily treated with some over-the-counter antacids purchased at the gift shop and washed down by bottled water. No coffee today.

Anyone watching me, as I moved up in line to buy a scone, would not have suspected that I was using a psychological technique; they would have seen some guy staring intently at the pastries, most likely very hungry.

That day I learned something new about pain control and awareness of bodily sensations, and I fully realized that this technique was useful for more than just managing anxiety. I have written elsewhere about more targeted methods for pain management. But it was good to have a grounding method available—one that could take me to a neutral place—when I found myself panicked by a troubling sensation in my stomach and chest. When my anxious feeling got too big I was unable to hear the signal, a signal of real pain, and reacted with fear and the physiological pattern of arousal associated with anxiety.

One of my next chances, still early on, to use the 54321 Technique was another plane trip I took, this time to another country. I travel a lot, and I was in a very rural part of India, traveling with a couple of friends. We were sleeping in small cots with mosquito nets, and in the part of rural desert India where we were visiting, there was no electricity. It was so isolated there did not even seem to be any animals, much less noise from the hubbub of civilization.

That night I dozed off to sleep, as did my companions, after briefly reading a novel by flashlight for a few minutes. The next thing I knew, I woke up in the middle of the night, to the persistent hum of a mosquito. Somehow it had gotten inside my mosquito net. I didn't want to use my flashlight, but eventually I had to use the light, in order to locate what had, by now, become my mortal enemy.

By the time I had vanquished my foe, I had also managed to get my adrenalin pumping like I was in an Olympic competition. When I laid back down, to go to sleep, I couldn't; I was too wound up.

It did not take long for me to decide to switch to a neutral gear, so I began to use the 54321 Technique. However, with my eyes open or eyes shut, there was just an identical pitch black; I couldn't see a difference. Without electricity there was just nothing to see.

Same with the sounds, it was absolutely quiet. *What to do*?

So I got creative. I used five things I saw earlier that day...five things I heard that day, etc...and it worked like a charm. During that trip I tried several variations and figured out you can use things you remember just as easily—or perhaps more so—than things in the 'here and now', as long as they are compelling enough to absorb your attention. Now, you can't just remember them, you have to re-experience them sort of like a flashback, only a positive flashback. You have to *be here now*, only, instead you go back to the past to *be there then*.

When I got back from that vacation, I shared my newfound discovery with one of my trauma patients, a pharmacist at my hospital. She had been using the technique for some time with good success, to manage her flashbacks and anxiety, and I was eager to share with her what I had discovered: that the technique does not have to focus on the present (the mindfulness component) but that memories could work equally well, as long as they were re-experienced not just remembered.

This patient instantly saw the potential more clearly than I had seen it. It is one of the perks of being a therapist—if you work collaboratively, you can count on your patients to teach you a great deal. When she learned from me that the 54321 would work just as well with memories, her eyes lit up.

She asked me, with joyful anticipation, "You mean, I can use my grandmother's jams?" Her favorite grandmother had died several years earlier, and she remembered this loved matriarch not only as a great source of comfort and security, but also as exceptionally skilled in the kitchen. Her grandmother's wonderful home-made jams were only a memory. But for this client, the memory of these jams was a compellingly satisfying one. It was, for her, a memory that was far more absorbing, and very effective.

These types of discoveries taught me, my colleagues, and my clients that if we distract ourselves by reliving key memories, then these powerfully interesting memories can easily take us away from unwanted fears and anxiety.

By the time a person reaches adulthood, they have a store of powerful memories that they can learn to tap in to, at any time. Once you know to look for them, you will discover that inside your head is a vast reservoir of these very key resources.

You can use these peak memories one at a time, to give yourself some instant diversion, or you can use them—in a modified 54321 Technique—to powerfully manage your feelings.

Applying this memory-based adaptation to modify the 54321 Technique is easy. First, you need to practice with the senses, in the here and now, making use of the mindfulness component to build up your basic skill. However, once you have mastered that basic skill, and can use it with ease, you can also try instead to focus on reliving sensory experiences from the recent past.

The real power in this technique, however, comes when you make it yours, and instead use some of your own most cherished experiences, from any time in your past. You can pick, for the three categories, anything that you find compelling. Don't worry about which senses are involved, in this version. It's not about the senses, although of course we do use them. In using this technique, you only need to use the senses to master the basic technique and to grasp the need for attending to three distinct kinds of things (categories). To use this technique with past memories it is fine to have, instead, three different kinds of memories. For example, one category for the aforementioned client, might be tasty things her grandmother baked or cooked. A second category for her might be fun vacation experiences, and a third category could be the pets she has loved.

She could then start with her grandmother's cupcakes, biscuits, jams, soups and barbecue. Then she could relive sitting in the hammock in Jamaica, the sauna at that resort, the road trip she took when she first got her license, and the feel of the supportive ocean as she floated on her back. Then she could attend to five things she did with her golden retriever. Of course once she had noticed five from each of the three categories, she could go back to find four things from Grandma, etc. It is still important to have three categories of distinct things, in order to get the benefit of intensified absorption from fractionation.

Everyone's favorite memories can differ. You might not even remember your grandmother (or not fondly) and, if your life has been hard, you might protest that you don't have any good memories. These memories can take many forms. For a 16-year-old boy it might be five different rap songs, or five different times he was able to penetrate a zone defense. What matters is that you use a memory that YOU find interesting. Each person - with their differing interests - finds unique key memories, but we all have some. If you are so depressed that you can't think of *anything* good, that's just your depression speaking. You will have to look a little harder but there were some. Look for a time when your life was more interesting or fun, or times that stood out when you persisted or prevailed, even when things were really rough.

You don't just think about grandma's jams, you eat them. You don't remember the title of a favored song; you hear it - long enough to bring a smile or to get your feet tapping, before moving to the next memory.

Don't believe you can do that? Try this exercise:

Imagine there is a lemon in your fridge. Take the lemon in your hand. Feel it in with your fingers, its texture, and how cold it is. Smell it. Now, peel away some of the skin, hold it to your nose, and take a bite.

If your body can remember to salivate, with an imagined or remembered lemon, then it can also fully remember your peak moments, often better than you can. One vivid memory often reminds you of others long forgotten.

By the time I moved away from that log cabin in the Smokey Mountains (I now live and work in beautiful Charleston, S.C.), I had already found dozens of such key moments from my past, moments that I could make use of in this and similar techniques. I like to say I had a quiver full, since that was a time when most of my clients were Cherokee Indians.

I sometimes use these "arrows" one memory at a time. However, when I need the big gun tools, I use three separate types of key moments, still counting down 54321 in the manner of the basic technique. Of course, I also still use the basic senses at times. They are easy to do, and to remember to use, and very handy in a pinch.

You have my advance encouragement to teach the 54321 Technique to your friends and family. It is easy to teach, once you have practiced it a couple of times. I suggest you start by teaching them to use their senses, this is still the easiest way to teach 54321. There are many other variations on this technique, but they are advanced and outside the scope of this book.

Contraindications

Before we move next to breathing techniques, I want to mention a couple of drawbacks of this technique. First, it is a distraction technique, and as such may not be the best choice for a feeling signal that needs to be heeded. If you are in real physical danger, for example, then distracting yourself could be foolish. 54321 and other distraction techniques work best on erroneous signals. Another problem is that for phobias, urges, and compulsions, you can tend to make the urge or feeling stronger by finding one more way to escape. These are usually better treated with exposure-type interventions.

Chapter Two
Breathing Easy

Anxiety and Breathing Techniques

Anxiety and stress can make life a challenge. If you are an anxious person, or if you have panic attacks, you may have been told that it is "all in your head," but that is not true. In fact, the physical symptoms of anxiety are not only very real, but often these biological processes are the components of anxiety that are the most troublesome. Many of the most effective methods I use to help clients manage anxiety succeed because they impact the physical symptoms, such as heart rate, rapid breathing, shaky hands, muscle tension, and feelings of suffocation.

When a person is afraid, stressed, anxious, and

especially while having an anxiety attack, a physical survival mode has kicked in. They experience a number of manifestations that are physiological and even neuro-hormonal symptoms that often have little or no connection to what they are thinking. This set of physiological responses may well include a surge of stress-related chemicals like adrenaline and cortisol, a rapid heart rate, shallow but rapid breathing, tense muscles, shakiness, cold and sweaty hands and feet, and other anxiety symptoms associated with the fight or flight response syndrome (see Chapter Six for a more thorough discussion of that syndrome).

Breathing exercises like the ones I am discussing in this chapter are aimed at countering the above set of physical reactions. The physical symptoms that can get you keyed up like a cat on a hot tin roof are all too familiar. They are actually hard wired biophysiological changes that are useful as a survival mechanism. But when you are reacting like you are being chased by a tiger (when there isn't a tiger, much less anything you can fix right now), then this group of physical changes are cumbersome and scary.

Fortunately, you also have a parallel nervous system that counters the survival response, and just as there are a bundle of symptoms and functions that are designed to help you escape an adversary, there are a number of automatic processes, that, if engaged, can unwind you just as well. These are called parasympathetic functions. Deep breathing (as opposed to the rapid shallow breathing of the survival response) is one such process. Another is relaxation of your muscles. There are several others. Any one of them, when used with understanding and skill, can help you relax. Some of the most effective grounding techniques I employ when dealing with anxiety are these physical processes that we all know, but do not routinely use to our advantage.

Breathing in a deep and nourishing manner is one way to mobilize this parallel system of physical responses. If you engage one of the parasympathetic functions the others can, and often will, cascade down with it. By changing your breathing response, the whole system of related reactions can also dampen down, de-escalate, and unwind. Slow, deep breathing is one of the easiest methods you can use to unleash your body's relaxation response, and to reverse the amped-up physical syndrome that accompanies anxiety and stress.

The Art of Breathing

The kind of breathing you need to learn, to better manage your anxiety, is a deep, slow breathing that makes use of the muscles of the diaphragm. Learning to manage anxiety involves some of the same skills that a singer develops, if the singer wishes to hold a note for a long time.

Breathing is also mandated training for an actor, who needs to take in enough air that he can project loudly from the stage, in his "stage voice." Swimmers also learn it, gymnasts need it, as do Special Forces service personnel.

Actors and singers often take voice lessons, while persons dealing with anxiety often learn to breathe by going to a psychologist or reading self-help books on anxiety management. The lesson is pretty much the same. In both cases, you learn to exercise an often unused muscle. The diaphragm is a muscle area just above and just below the lower ribs, near the lower underused portion of your lungs. When you are breathing deeply, you use this muscle and lung area to inhale fully, instead of breathing only in the chest area. This skill improves with practice. Singers recognize that the lung can act as a bellows and is a crucial part of the instrument that is their voice. They pay good money and practice long hours to get their "instrument" up to par. If you have a tendency towards excessive anxiety, you need to put in a similar amount of effort at learning how to breathe deeply.

Most people breathe with their chest, and they breathe with shallow rapid breaths. When they become anxious this shallow rapid breathing is very exaggerated, almost like a dog panting after a good hard run. Your goal is to learn to breathe deep into the bottom of your lungs, using the diaphragm muscle instead of just breathing rapidly in your chest. The closest natural thing that resembles what I am describing is a deep sigh.

To familiarize yourself with this process, you should start by putting your hand on your stomach, just at or below the bottom of your rib cage, where the diaphragm muscle is located. Put another hand on your chest. Now see if you can try breathing in a way that fills the lower lungs more, pushing that hand out more fully than the one on the chest, as you breathe.

It is easier to practice initially with the guidance of a therapist, (or singing coach!) but most people can easily learn this on their own or using an online breathing app. Ideally, you can practice this kind of breathing initially in private, at a time when your anxiety is not at its peak. Once the skill becomes almost second nature, it can be deployed as a method for interrupting or countering the "keyed up" anxiety and stress responses.

In this chapter I want to introduce two of the most widely shared breathing techniques. I would share with you who developed them, but I have not been able to find the source to give credit. Maybe the cavemen first developed them, in order to unwind after escaping a saber-tooth and before dinner.

Four Square or *Box Breathing*

Early on, before you have mastered the art and

skill of slow and relaxed deep breathing, it's good to have some structure or scaffolding for what you are learning. There is no one "right" way to breathe deeply. The two methods I am introducing are only suggestions, and if you already have a way of breathing that you learned, for example as a meditation, or in some kind of Yoga, feel free to add the things that worked for you in to this process. The techniques I am teaching are suggestions, and best modified to suit you. They are not spiritual or meditative, so it doesn't matter which nostril you use—they are simply exercises that help with your health.

One easy way to teach a method of deeper breathing, *four square* or *box breathing*, is a good way to learn the basics. It is not a big stretch for those who have let their diaphragm muscle atrophy from lack of use.

Four square or *box breathing* is an exercise that will give you some practice at breathing almost twice as deeply as you do when you are getting anxious. It is easy to remember, and can be done by almost anyone. It is especially suited to rank beginners, as it does not require much diaphragm strength or rigorous practice. If you were working out, this would be the equivalent of starting to lift weights with the smallest size.

In *four square* breathing or *box breathing*, you count to four each of four times, about a second or so for each number of the count. The idea is to make a square. Count slowly to four while breathing in (1, 2, 3, 4), then hold for another side of the square, (hold your breath for another count of four), then while breathing out, count again to four, and fourthly, count to four one more time while holding, before you breathe in. Repeat the cycle by breathing in again, going around all four sides; you typically should do these a number of times. If you are anxious and trying to turn on the relaxation response, you can do this until it works.

Most people find this easy to do and easier still

to remember. While it does not lead to the really deep and profoundly relaxed breathing, it is sufficiently deep to interrupt the more shallow rapid breaths (often just about 1, 2, 1, 2) that are characteristic of the fight or flight phenomena.

Seven Eleven Breathing

A deeper breathing exercise, and one that is closer to the kind of breathing that singers use, is known as *seven eleven*. Again these numbers are guidelines (as is the 4 in *box breathing*). If you do not like odd numbers or have something against convenience stores, you might prefer 8-12 or 6-10.

Seven eleven is a little harder to do if you have neglected your diaphragm muscle and that muscle has become atrophied or weak. The deeper breathing that the *seven eleven* technique calls for requires a bit more muscle tone in the diaphragm. So this exercise also takes some serious practice to master well.

In the *seven eleven* breathing technique, you count slowly to seven while breathing in. (As slowly as "one thousand one, one thousand two," etc., but you do not need to be that precise.) While breathing out, you slowly count to 11 before repeating the cycle. Repeat until you no longer feel the need (usually less than 5 or 6 minutes).

Some Modifications of These Techniques

Modifications of these two techniques are often useful to strengthen the impact and change it to your own liking. Some people suggest while doing breathing exercises for anxiety, you breathe in through the nose and then breathe out through the mouth. More advanced yoga techniques might have you inhaling through one nostril and out another. While these modifications are not necessary, and likely have more to do with meditation or spiritual practices than health *per se*, if you find one of them helpful, you should consider adopting or adapting it.

Others find it useful to combine this with a peaceful focused thought, or to focus on a restful or healthy image. That thought or image could be an additional source of comfort, if it is already meaningful to you. You can pick a word that for you means "relax!', for instance "calm," "peace," "one," and say that word to yourself as you breathe out. Religions and other spiritual practices often have their own storehouse of words, quotes, koans, or practices like a rosary, that evoke their preferred type of serenity or tranquility.

Clients with an aptitude for processing with a visual mode can find creative visualization can be helpful to strengthen the effects of breathing. If you have a favorite color that is especially evocative of calmness or relaxation, then you might find it helpful or calming to accompany the intake with an image or sensation that this color is spreading into your lungs or throughout your body. Others have found it helpful to imagine a peaceful scene that brings them comfort and peace while they breathe deeply.

One very effective way to make the breathing technique more powerful is to combine it with another relaxation technique, such as tensing and relaxing muscles. In a very simple version of this modification, you can squeeze the muscles in your hands and forearms, tensing them as you breathe in, and then gradually relax the same muscles as you breathe out. If you are already familiar with progressive relaxation techniques you can be more creative with this modification. A word of caution: spend more effort relaxing than tensing. The idea is to switch on the parasympathetic nervous system (see Chapter Six) and tensing muscles in progressive relaxation is more about finding the muscle than tensing it.

Yoga, Tai Chi, and various types of meditation might also be helpful ways to bolster the relaxation response for those who are drawn to these methods. Indeed, these and related techniques have long been a cornerstone of health in ancient cultures of the world, and are only beginning to be woven into western ideas about health. The Serenity Prayer has also been a useful meditation from the Christian Tradition:

> "God, give us grace to accept with serenity
> the things that cannot be changed,
> Courage to change the things
> which should be changed,
> and the Wisdom to distinguish
> the one from the other."

When to Use Deep Breathing

Deep breathing is easy to learn and easy to do without being noticed if you are in public; therefore, it is a good habit to instill in your weekly routine. Deep breathing can play a central role in keeping your overall level of stress and anxiety manageable. While it can be helpful at any stage, it works especially well as an anxiety management tool in the early stages of a spiral of anxious feelings. However, because hyperventilation plays such a central role in panic attacks, many find that some skilled version of breathing control helps especially well in the midst of hyperventilation.

Panic attacks and hyperventilating are a whole other topic and discussed in more depth in Chapter 6. One of the key contributors to panic attacks and hyperventilation is the anxious type of breathing that is the hallmark of anxiety (shallow rapid breaths). When an anxious person breathes in a panicky, rapid, shallow type of breathing, that process leads to an imbalance in body chemicals that can be reversed with deep breathing. Without going into the complicated physiology discussed at the end of this book, the two techniques I have introduced have a component built in to their structure that makes them especially useful if you are dealing with a panic attack, or trying to avoid one. For now, take my word for it that if you breathe in deeply but have (like in *seven eleven*) more breath out than in, this can reverse or even ward off a panic attack, if sustained for several minutes.

Everyone knows to take a deep breath in a daunting situation, but if you have practiced this, and you have built up your diaphragm muscle, several deep breaths can be much more powerful when supported by a strong diaphragm. You can use breathing to steady yourself, like the sniper does before he pulls a trigger, or the basketball player at the free throw line. SWAT teams are often trained to take at least one deep breath before kicking in the door. In the movie based on the book *American Sniper* (Kyle, McEwan, and Defelice, 2012), the film actually depicted the practice visually in a manner that was inaccurate, but the voice of the protagonist early in the movie reflects the book more accurately, and how breathing is actually employed by the Special Forces at times like that. A sniper cannot afford to have his hand shake, so by breathing in deeply, a soldier can switch on the relaxation response, and warm up his hands. (The sympathetic nervous system drains the blood and cold hands shiver, so a switch to relaxing mode is needed.)

These techniques can be learned on your own, but to be most effective you may need to adjust them to suit you better. For example when I first tried *box breathing*, I found that I had to make a triangle rather than a square, because I could not hold my breath that long before breathing in again. (Four in, hold for a count of four, and four out, making it a triangle rather than a square or box). It worked just as well.

A skilled therapist can often spot more easily the mistakes you are making and help you refine the technique if it isn't working right for you.

Practice is fairly important in any grounding technique, including breathing. The goal is not just to have good muscle tone in your diaphragm, it is to develop new habits, including taking at least one deep breath when faced with a precarious or stressful situation, and more if the situation is severe. Combined with other resources and other grounding techniques, breathing can be a very useful tool as part of your effort at overcoming and managing anxiety.

Chapter Three
Worries That Work

In the first two chapters I introduced techniques that can be helpful in more severe types of anxiety (like flashbacks that are often a consequence of trauma, or severe anxiety attacks). Breathing is also helpful with milder anxiety and with worries. However, in this chapter I wanted to discuss some ways to deal with the kinds of worries and fretting that are daily burdens to the terminally anxious person. I hope to provide the reader with some ideas that can be helpful in curbing or minimizing this more chronic worrying.

A caveat before proceeding: you will need a whole different set of tools if you are dealing with even mild obsessions or compulsions, much less a full blown Obsessive Compulsive Disorder. It is beyond the scope of this book to discuss these in the depth they deserve, so for now please note that a more cognitive behavioral approach to obsessions and compulsions is usually the most effective. I cover these concepts more fully in my upcoming book on *Special Topics in Anxiety*.

Some worry may be useful, and certainly can be a normal spare time activity, but typically the people who tend to worry are often those who worry way too much. While some of these people have been diagnosed with an anxiety disorder, and seek some form of treatment, most chronic worriers never seek help. They just assume that they will always be tormented by their worries and take that predicament as a fact of life. The ideas presented in this chapter provide some options for people who suffer from chronic worries. The program outlined below, even in part, can be helpful, provided that you can customize it to your specific situation.

Of course, if you are already following the advice of Meher Baba (1967)—popularized in a song by Bobby McFerrin—and you already subscribe to the "Don't Worry, Be Happy," carefree mantra, you can skip this chapter.

Despite all the effort and time invested, worriers often find that they do not worry very effectively. If they did, of course, they would not have to keep worrying, or could at least move on to some newer and more pressing worries. This chapter can help worriers to harness some of that hamster wheel energy and focus it, instead, on solving some of the problems that they have been worrying about.

The key to this process begins with you. You have to decide that you are serious about tackling your problems, and not just accept the need to be worrying about them for worry's sake, in an endless and nonproductive loop. While this chapter is not aimed at resolving all of life's problems, and these problems and the worry can be very painful, it makes solutions to your worries more likely, at least for those problems that you can do something about. You need to develop a framework for more effective worry.

Step One- Scheduling the Work of Worry

Worrying 24/7 is not only exhausting, but it keeps you from being effective, having fun, and living a more full and rewarding life. When problems loom, the chronic worrier will let those problems consume them. The higher the stakes, of course, the more your worrying takes over your consciousness. Worry can keep sleep at arm's length, and fill your body with muscle tension, adrenaline, and cortisol (a stress hormone that among other things increases belly fat). Your worries can crowd out any enjoyable leisure time, since it leaves too little time for more pleasurable pastimes.

Ask yourself, "Do you really need to worry most of the day and all of the bedtime hours?" The answer, if you are candid, is "no." It makes no sense to worry all the time, because if that worked, you would have solved all of these worries, given all the time you have already invested. But what would happen if you schedule your worry time, setting aside specific days or times to do the work of worry, so it can free up the rest of your day? Of course this scheduling of your worries will work *only* if you resolve to give it your all during the time you set aside to do the work of worry. If you pledge to put at least as much effort (not time, *effort*) into the scheduled worry time as you would otherwise, then you can, in good conscience, let the worries go, for most of the other hours of your day.

If you take this scheduling idea seriously, you can stop worrying all the time, and start worrying in a more focused and effective way. More importantly, eventually you will train yourself to be able to worry mostly at a time and place of your choosing.

The idea is to initially put aside about twenty to thirty minutes a day, for no more than six days a week, to do the work of worry. For those who are religious, you may want to set aside, (and not do the work of worry at all) a day of rest that is prescribed by your faith. For everybody, it's advisable to have at least one day off from worry, preferably on a weekend, for rest or for enjoyment. If you had a favorite day when you were growing up (mine was Saturday) that would be an especially good day to reclaim for more fun and little or no worry.

On the day off, and other times outside the scheduled time for worry, whenever a worry grabs your attention put it aside and tell yourself something along the lines of "I will deal with that at the appointed time" or simply "not now." Others might prefer "later" or a more colorful phrase. If you mean what you are saying, when you say it to yourself, then you will find that most worries can wait until you are ready to tackle them.

If this cannot be implemented, you may be one of those people who use worry and thinking as a way of distracting yourself from uncomfortable feelings; better to have your head doing a hamster wheel than feel that pumping heart and tight chest. This might more profitably be dealt with in therapy where a psychologist could help you manage your feelings more comfortably. Obsessions also can serve a similar role, and make worry work more challenging.

When To Do the Work Of Worry

OK, so it is time to schedule an appointment with yourself to work on worrying about your problems. Ideally, you should make the appointment to do the worry work at about the same time each day.

Figure out when you worry the most, and

maybe you can start then. If you are someone who lays in bed tossing and turning and can't shut the worries off, then maybe that is the time, since it would be lost time anyway (only maybe don't use the bed). Set aside a specific time to do the work of worry, such as just before bedtime, or when you get off of work. Of course any time of day is good, but keep in mind that worry can be rather draining.

Your worry work time should be scheduled at an easy-to-remember time, lasting for a specified interval. It is probably good to set aside at least half an hour initially. If you take this task seriously and with sincere intention, this interval is, with rare exceptions, the only significant time you have set aside to indulge in worry, so make it long enough that you won't feel like you are being a slacker. Later, when you get good at the work of worry, you can do the work in 15-20 minutes or less, and by then you may only take a few days a week for the work of worry. The plan is to take your worry as a prompt to do something, literally to turn the process of worrying into action and problem solving.

If you have a planner or calendar that you normally use, block out the time and don't double schedule yourself. If you are not that organized, put a note to yourself on the fridge, as a reminder. If you have family or friends who may want to interrupt, tell them you need that time as "me time." If you truly must miss an appointed worry time, then have a plan to add that time (as a makeup time) to the next session. Be honest with yourself. You can't fool yourself to postpone the worry if you know you will ditch the appointed worry session.

I don't recommend that you use a 3:00 a.m. time slot, unless you are truly a night owl. If you are worrying most in those early morning hours, and you are waking up in order to worry, then there is a chance you have other serious problems, especially if you can't get back to sleep.

You could, with this pattern, be having trouble with sleep because you are clinically depressed. (Early morning wakening is a key symptom of clinical depression.) If this "early morning wakening" is not a lifelong habit, then diagnosing and then addressing the depression, if that is what it is, would be a high priority. At that time of morning anxiety can also reflect night terrors, nightmares, or flashbacks from trauma, not to mention physiological disorders. You may be waking up from troubled dreams, and when that is the case, the anxiety often reflects the dream content, which may or may not always be a conscious worry. If it is anxiety from a dream or a flashback, try a breathing technique or a distraction technique like the 54321 exercise introduced in the first chapter.

Step 2 - Setting Up Your Worry Nook

Before you start, you will want to pick a place,

and arrange the setting so you can do the work of worry. Ideally it will be a place that allows you to be alone, and to not be disturbed. It could be a favorite chair, or a bathroom (bubble baths can be nice), or any place that is quiet, but ideally you will be able to sit quite comfortably, and yet not so comfortably that you will fall asleep there.

If the scheduled time is during the day, you will need to turn off the phone, especially the cell phone (including the text alert), or at least put it out of hearing range. One client used the breadbox to stow the phone. Anything else that might distract you, like a TV, laptop, or computer, should also be turned off, silenced, and out of reach.

Now, in addition, there are some aids that you might want to have, depending on how you tend to go about transforming worries into problems that you can solve. You might want to have handy either a small blackboard with chalk, or a bulletin board with pins. Instead of, or in addition to these tools, some people prefer putting their thoughts and musings in a journal or even a scrapbook. You also need plenty of paper and a pen or sharpened pencil, and maybe some index cards.

Finally, you may want to have one or two things in your worry nook that can provide you a sense of comfort. Hot chocolate? Something to remind you of a time in your life when you felt more confidant and worry-free. It could be anything—an old photo, a keepsake, a newspaper clipping, an award, or a page from a magazine that evokes a sense of comfort, confidence and effectiveness. You mean business, and are getting ready to tackle your worries.

The important thing, is that your worry nook needs to be a place you can feel relatively free of mental clutter, so you can bring all your resources to bear upon the problems.

Step 3- Making Your Worries Work For You

The first step in the work of worry is to make sure that no worry goes unnoticed. As they run through your head, try to notice them, but do not try to solve them, or stop them. When you are ready you can start to jot them down. For the early efforts, the main goal is to make an exhaustive accounting of problems that cause you to worry. Be as specific as possible and leave no stone unturned. Do not try to prioritize or make this a typical "to do" list at this stage, just be sure that you can honestly say to yourself that you have it more or less all down. Many of my chronic anxiety patients are surprised that just dumping it all on paper gives them more relief than they could have imagined. Add to this list as necessary, should you forget something important or if new worries pop up. This is not about crossing things off the list, it's about being confident that you are about to address most or all the worries over the coming days.

Avoid using general statements, and instead be as specific as possible. Suppose you are worried about having been recently ticketed for Driving Under the Influence (DUI). That's a pretty big worry, but conceived in that way, it is typically too big to deal effectively with. Breaking that down into smaller, more specific worries, would be an excellent first step.

Here are some specific worries that might be associated with a DUI:

- Should I get a lawyer?
- How to find a good lawyer.
- How to pay for a lawyer.
- How to pay court costs and fines.
- Can I get a plea bargain?
- Will I go to jail?
- Will I lose my license?
- Will I lose my insurance?
- How can I get to work if I can't drive?

- How much will my insurance go up?
- What if my boss finds out? Can this impact my job?
- How bad is my drinking problem?
- Should I get counseling for alcohol? If so, where?
- What should I tell my family?
- Can I get a work waiver?

As you can see, big worries often include a whole boatload of smaller, related worries. One of the ways worries can grab hold of you and hang on is that when you start to turn your attention to one, another pops up and says "no don't forget about me, what about (fill in the blank)." This can be overwhelming, and the approach I am suggesting of getting it all down and as specifically as possible, takes away the frantic sense that you might be missing a potential threat.

At first, do not make any effort to organize the worries, and don't worry about which ones you need to think about first, or deal with first. Just be exhaustive.

After a session (or several) of this list making, you should have pretty much identified nearly all of your most pressing problems and concerns. Now in between the appointed worry sessions, if your mind goes to one of these worries, you can honestly tell yourself, "I've got it, it's already on the list" or "Now is not an effective time. I will deal with it with a laser focus later."

Now is when we turn to problem solving. You may already have an effective method for problem solving, and if you do, then that approach would be a good place to start. The main thing I ask is that whatever method you use, try to bring your "A" game, which typically means a laser focus (with an absorption in the process that rivals the kind of "being in the zone" you find with a gold medalist). You are only devoting a few minutes, but in return you are going to really get down to work now.

If you do not already have a system for problem solving that works, you can employ one of many techniques that help (Jones, 2009; Stracker 1997). While it is beyond the scope of the current chapter to teach problem solving, a few observations about how to proceed will be helpful in finding the right mix of approaches.

First and foremost, the strategy that is best for you is the one that works for you. If you have tried making a list, or some other technique, and it has worked, by all means build on that, but if it has never worked, then there is a good chance you will get the same bad result. Lists can be helpful for many people who are detail oriented but they often boomerang and make some anxious and depressed persons feel helpless (or lazy, or not competent), because you do not cross enough off your list. The same can be true for other commonly-used approaches like prioritizing.

As we will discuss further in Chapter Five on thinking, people who tend to be anxious also make some characteristic thinking errors, and one is to make mountains out of molehills, and a related one is to bite off more than you can chew. If you tend to make the first mistake, then you need to identify more accurately what the problem is, in a way that a reasonable person might view it. If you feel your money problems are so bad that it's only a matter of time before you are "ruined" then you probably are guilty of making the problem so big no one could solve it. Maybe you should first figure out basics like how to make the bills this month, or even make up a new, more realistic budget. Even better, start with losing the concept of "ruined," it's pretty likely to ruin you if you keep thinking like that.

The related problem of biting off more than you can chew is especially problematic for people who are feeling dread, anxiety, and helplessness. In normal circumstances, when life is good and all is well, it can be a good idea to reach a little beyond your grasp, as it can motivate you to dream and strive for the stars. But if you are feeling depleted and overwhelmed, and those feelings stop you from even trying to solve a problem, then the first thing you need to do is put a stop to feeling so overwhelmed. The solution to that is usually for you to break the problem into smaller but doable first steps. Ask yourself what can you do today (or this afternoon) that will give you a start on this problem (or move you forward a little). Some anxious or depressed patients may have to make it an even smaller step, like "What can I do in the next ten minutes?" It has to be a step in the right direction, and a step you can take today, not this week.

One of my clients likened this process to driving in a fog. You should lower your headlight beam to the road in front of you, and only drive forward in the part you can see. You don't want to drive in the part you can't see, but even if you just go a few feet at a time, you eventually drive out of the fog.

When it comes to prioritizing, one mistake a lot of people make is it to tackle the most important or pressing problem first. While that can work, it is not for everyone. For people who are chronically worried or helpless, such a disheartening choice leads as often as not to paralysis and failure, and because of that failure, to even more helplessness and worry. Let's say you have three credit cards, where you owe money, and on one you owe $200 at a 12% interest rate, another you owe $450 at a 19% rate, and a third you owe $3000 at a 21% rate.

Logic and good economics would suggest you should pay off the bill where you pay the highest interest rate first, and pay the minimum on the others. However, for many people who feel anxious, the low hanging fruit might be the better place to start. If you could actually pay off one of the three cards, the increase in self confidence that results typically more than outweighs the small loss from paying the lower rate off first.

Index cards are a helpful aid, especially when you are easily distracted. If you write one smaller, specific worry each on an index card, you can keep coming back until you get it done. You can sort them into piles of cards that all seem to go together. You might find it useful to sort them into "things I have no control over," and "things I can do something about." The latter pile can then be sorted into "urgent" and "whenever" piles, and the urgent cards into easiest and hardest. A "hard and urgent" pile may still need some breaking up into smaller steps.

Once you have selected a problem small enough that it might realistically be solved soon, you can resolve to address it then. If you can solve it during the appointed worry time, that's OK, otherwise plan to address it outside the time you have set aside for worry. In this way you can begin to whittle away at your problems, gradually bringing them under control, and giving yourself a series of small wins that start to add up.

Not all problems can be broken down into smaller ones that can be addressed in one day, but most actually can. One big problem may eventually lead to eight or nine smaller problems that can be solved.

You may also need to identify the barriers to your success. See if there is some way to chip away at that barrier, or work around it. What are these barriers? One of the bigger barriers for most of us is not enough money, or other resource challenges like transportation or time. For some of us, there are also health barriers, toxic relationships, or disabilities, to name some of the more frequent challenges.

Some of these barriers can't be changed, and you may have to learn how to accept them, but acceptance comes more readily when you know you have tried everything you can think of to overcome them. That does not mean you can't find ways to work around them. If a guitarist who loses his arm can learn to play with his feet, there is probably a way to work around your barrier, although it may take some time or a different perspective, before you figure it out. Therapists are especially good at giving you a new perspective and seeing side exits you may have missed.

For the harder problems, especially, it can be very helpful for you to journal or write in a notebook about it, perhaps listing the pros and cons. For the biggest problems it can even be helpful to externalize it, by giving it a name. You might call the biggest one the Monkey on My Back or the Tasmanian Bill Bully, and if you have a more specific name, that's even better. Externalizing your problem, also called decentering, symbolically takes the problem outside of you; as such, it makes it easier to act on it.

Don't forget to use the creative side of your brain. Many problems which feel stuck are feeling that way because you are using the wrong skillset. Some problems lend themselves to logical solutions but many times the best answer takes into account several things like feelings and creativity in addition to logic. If you are artistic you might want to draw or sketch the problem, or portray it in some other creative way. You might also sketch or draw any barriers as well. This can help to engage the creative side of your brain. Many problems that cannot be solved logically are amenable to a solution that relies on the non-logical but creative side of our brain. Go ahead and be creative, make a dartboard with the bull's eye having a picture of the goal (or a barrier if you prefer). Use physical materials like a bulletin board or blackboard to put the problem in front of you and make it more tangible.

Now you have all the problems before you,

and you have them broken down into solvable portions. Once you have solved the easier ones move on to the harder ones. As you get more confident that there are actually solutions within your grasp, the process becomes almost second nature.

Sometimes the anxiety or panic takes over, and that can get in the way. If this happens to you during your appointed worry time, chances are, not much will get done in the remaining 20 minutes. Focus instead on taming the anxiety, riding it out, or at least rolling it back using one of the techniques in this book. The 54321 Technique I describe in Chapter One can be useful at these times, by grounding yourself in your senses. Take a deep breath. Stretch your legs for a minute. Or maybe use some mindfulness to quell the turmoil.

You are not, of course, always going to be able to solve your problems by yourself. A therapist can help you sort out the more challenging ones.

Another set of eyes can help. If not a therapist, a good friend may have a new perspective.

When you have begun to use the work of worry more effectively, you can make it a more routine part of your life. Cut the frequency of the worry work down to two or three times a week, and this becomes easier and easier as you get confident about putting worries on hold routinely. This can be done if you know full well that you will get to them soon, and with a laser focus. If you have a tendency to procrastinate, then that will also have to be addressed. Learn to replace worries with plans or with problem solving. To do this effectively you may need to use the Cognitive Behavioral techniques discussed in Chapter Five to retrain some negative and counterproductive thoughts.

Chapter Four
Defusing Fears and Anxiety

The exposure techniques introduced in this chapter, *desensitization* (done either through fantasy or in the real-world), and more extreme kinds, often in the form of *Implosion* or *flooding,* can both be helpful for taming unrealistic fears and phobias. Exposure methods are proven techniques that work for problems that range from phobias to more serious problems like flashbacks and PTSD. Whole books, of course, are written on these approaches, but in this chapter I wanted to at least introduce two of the main techniques that therapists may use, with the intention that you might be able to begin to figure out how to apply exposure to some of your own problems.

Sensitization

Sensitization is a word that describes what happens when we learn to associate a feeling, like anxiety, with a particular situation. While this can be useful when your learning has been accurate (a fear of rattlesnakes can for example, be a useful fear), much of this conditioned learning can be unrealistic, and even border on the superstitious. When a Veteran of Afghanistan learns that a loud noise may mean an IED and that his buddies are in danger, that learning can directly impact survival in Iraq. But the same learning may not translate to a realistic fear in the USA, and the soldier's reaction many not play as well in Peoria, when a car backfires.

This specific example about the vet is called a flashback, but phobias and addictive urges are developed in a very similar manner. Phobias often arise when a situation becomes connected with danger, at least in the limbic system and hippocampus of the person with the phobia. However, when no realistic danger persists, but the anxiety still remains (in spades), then the phobia or unrealistic fear becomes entrenched in a manner that is not helpful. It will remain entrenched until you learn differently.

In such situations, if you become *sensitized* to a predicament, then you still feel that same reaction, even when that fear is actually no longer relevant. After that, being in the same or a similar situation or even thinking about that situation, can leave you feeling anxious, or generate a panic reaction.

For example, if you were riding on the freeway during rush hour, and you were involved in a serious motoring accident, you might develop a phobia about driving, especially about driving on the freeway during rush hour. This could be serious, if you need to drive to get to work, or when you need to take the freeway but won't even consider it.

Desensitization

Psychologists and other therapists have figured out how to help in these situations. *Desensitization* is the process by which you unlearn the connection between anxiety or fear and the situation that evokes it. For this unlearning to occur, you need to enter into the anxiety provoking situation—which is easier said than done—and relearn a more realistic picture. If there is no subsequent danger, you can then eventually come to recognize (and believe) that there is no longer anything to fear.

The techniques for managing anxiety that are discussed in this chapter are all variations on exposure therapy. Exposure therapy relies upon repetition of new, more accurate learning. If you can repeat a troubling situation (or the fantasied version of it) and no harm comes, the association eventually breaks down (the association is said to be extinguished, like a fire extinguisher).

However, you should be forewarned: these intense feelings do not go away without a fight. There is usually at least one moment in this process that the fear escalates, often bigger than it ever was before, as if it wants one last chance to convince you of the horrible danger, before it gives up and recedes. If you can learn to hang in there at these times, harrowing as they may feel, once you have learned to ride out one or two of these extinction bursts, success is usually close at hand.

There are basically two ways that you can use exposure techniques, and some clients prefer the scary way (*flooding* or *implosion*), and others are temperamentally inclined to take it all a bit more gradually (*systematic desensitization*).

First, let's talk about the hard way. One of the first examples of this approach was described by Wolpe (1958, 1970) who treated a teenage girl who had become terrified of cars after she was in a very scary accident. Wolpe required the girl to get into the car, and then the hysterically terrified girl was driven around in that car for several hours. Painful and scary as it was, her anxiety gradually abated, and by the time she was released from the car, she was no longer afraid (not even of Wolpe).

This technique, in its severest form, is known as *flooding,* and it was introduced and formalized as a behavioral technique by a psychologist named Stampfl (1967). Modern incarnations of this are techniques often also referred to as *in vivo* (i.e. live) interventions, where an individual is exposed to the aversive situation, often for a few sessions or even one long several-hour session. This is actually a proven technique, one that is considered an evidence-based treatment— meaning a treatment form that is proven to work. It seems to work effectively with animal phobias and it is also recognized as an effective intervention for fears associated with obsessions and compulsions. *In vivo* therapy is not always flooding and can be done more gradually but the more aggressive flooding-type therapies are usually *in vivo*.

While daunting, and not the cup of tea of most therapists (or patients), those who participate in *in vivo* desensitization by *flooding* interventions find that hanging out with the fear for a prolonged interval, yet with no adverse consequences, serves to "unlearn" the fear connection, and the anxiety desensitizes rapidly and effectively, once the fear habituates. It turns out you can get used to almost anything.

The term *systematic desensitization* is used to describe a careful, systematic approach to implementing *desensitization*, typically in a gradual and measured manner. This technique can be done *in vivo* (live in the real world), or— as Joseph Wolpe realized in 1973—much or even all of the therapy can be done in an armchair, using imaginary situations and imagined consequences. If you are looking for self-help techniques to use with your anxiety, these armchair approaches may be a good place to begin.

Exposure therapies that are designed to systematically desensitize encourage the individual to take a chance and enter into the feared situation. But while *flooding* or *implosive* types of *in vivo* interventions ask you to grab the bull by the horns, a more gradual approach is preferred by most clients and therapists.

The gradual exposure to a series of situations (individually tailored to be increasingly more anxiety-provoking) is called *systematic desensitization*. In this approach the client and therapist typically collaborate to develop a hierarchy of anxiety-provoking situations culminating in facing the most feared version of the problem. In the live version of this, the therapist accompanies the client and interacts with the targeted problem, but still gradually.

Systematic desensitization involves three steps.

- First, the client needs to learn how to relax, in a neutral situation, and become skilled at attaining a deep state of relaxation or grounding. The 54321 technique in Chapter One and breathing techniques in Chapter Two would help with this. Others may prefer to use self-hypnosis or a guided imagery technique, often with images of a safe place, and still others can use techniques that evoke a relaxation response like progressive muscle relaxation. The key here is to be able to evoke a calm and safe feeling, and hold on to those safe feelings while confronting the fearful situations. This safe and calm state is not used as an escape, a mistake many therapists have been known to make. Instead it is used as a means of keeping the anxious feeling in check (described in the third step below). Escape scenarios serve to make the anxiety worse.

- A second step is to generate a hierarchy of related anxiety-provoking situations. This means that you make a list of scenes that are related to the core fear or anxiety. These scenes must have varying degrees of perceived threat. You then arrange them in order from easiest to the hardest to face.

- In the third step you then work your way through the scenes, staying calm while mastering the easiest situation, and moving on to the next hardest scene, only when the earlier scenes are found to be manageable. The calm and peaceful state obtained in step one is maintained throughout, and serves to inhibit the anxious feeling, because it is generally true that you can't hold two contradictory feelings simultaneously.

In the live version you face each situation, starting with the easiest, and once that is mastered move on to the next. If you are afraid of driving on the interstate, you might first get comfortable with getting in your car and sitting, then with going around the block, and next, a ten minute drive through the neighborhood. By the time you get to the interstate, you might drive for only one exit, but soon you can be driving as much as you like, even in rush hour.

The imagination-driven armchair version works just the same, but you do it all in your mind. Sitting in a comfortable place, you first evoke the sense of peace and calm, and then—in your imagination—face the first and easiest challenge. You of course need to have worked out the hierarchy in advance, as making it up on the fly can be hard.

The evidence of treatment success behind the imagination-based version is not as compelling, probably because not everyone has the talent of fantasizing vividly, or for that matter of evoking and sustaining a reliably calm and serene state. I also assume some of that failure comes with less skilled therapists who use the safe imagery or feeling as an escape hatch, thereby building greater anxiety. Again, a competent and experienced therapist can help you develop your hierarchy and navigate the escalation in a way that is more likely to work effectively.

Medication can sometimes help when combined with desensitization, as you can take a strong anti-anxiety drug and then navigate either an implosive exposure or a more gradual one. One problem with a medication approach is that you might be inclined to attribute the success, if any, to the medication (rather than to yourself) and come to believe that the medication is necessary. Of course the benzodiazepines and some other medications used can be habit-forming. The biggest problem, however, is that when the dose is sufficient, it often makes the anxiety largely inaccessible, and therefore it can be harder to evoke the scenarios.

Prolonged exposure therapy is a term used for

the kind of therapy that the Veteran's Administration (VA) tends to rely on for treatment of veterans who have PTSD. This is an approach that has a lot of research backing up that it works. In Prolonged Exposure Therapy, the client is encouraged to re-tell their traumatic experiences in the present tense, gradually desensitizing the fear-laden memories. PTSD, however, whether treated in the manner of the VA or more gradually and comprehensively, typically requires a skilled therapist and generally should not be done in a self-help context.

Some virtual reality modules and games have been developed to provide a more realistic exposure to warlike predicaments without having to go on the battlefield. These computer graphic intensive interventions are usually, for now, prohibitively expensive, at least for providers who would like to use them, but there is some indication that prices may be easing.

Eye Movement Desensitization Reprocessing

(EMDR) therapy (Shapiro 2001) does not typically emphasize the exposure therapy component, but it seems to play a central role. EMDR is a technique in which the client is asked to attend to an image, sound, or touch that the therapist uses to engage both the dominant and non-dominant side of the client's brain, while they attend to a fearful memory. It is frequently used not only for treating trauma but other anxiety disorders. However, in my limited experience with it, especially in dealing with acute trauma, the portion of the technique that involves "noticing" whatever image or thought comes is effective—at least in part—because of the role of exposure.

Similarly, some clinical uses of mindfulness, (Sears, Tirch, and Denton 2011) may largely be successful due to the exposure component.

Chapter Five
Thinking Clearly

Probably the gold standard psychotherapy treatment for anxiety and depression is therapy that is focused on how you think (cognition). There is good research that shows that Cognitive Behavioral Therapy (CBT, as this type of treatment is called), can prove to be quite helpful for managing anxiety and other emotional problems.

CBT works by helping you change some of your thoughts, especially thoughts that are toxic (likely to make you feel bad). If you can change a thought, that change will be able to impact how you feel and also how you behave whenever you have that thought. It turns out we think a lot of thoughts in a day (more than we realize) and many of these thoughts just pop into our head, and we treat them like gospel, whether or not they are true.

Among the pioneers of what is now considered Cognitive Behavioral Therapy were Aaron Beck and Albert Ellis. Ellis (1962) emphasized that you can have beliefs that, because they are irrational, create unnecessary emotional and behavioral problems. Like subsequent cognitive theorists, Ellis argued that thoughts (he emphasized beliefs) can have a negative impact on your feelings and behaviors. He stated that having negative beliefs, when they were not justified by the actual situation that you appraise, can lock you in an endless cycle of difficulties and misery.

Aaron Beck (1967) expanded the ideas to include any distorted thinking, not just beliefs, and emphasized negative "distortions" in thinking as a major factor in depression. Beck initially identified what he called a cognitive triad: negative views of yourself, your world, and your future, and noted that thoughts like these play a major role in causing and sustaining depression. The theory and practice of CBT is very applicable to several other disorders, but it is especially useful and pertinent in understanding and treating anxiety and depression.

I will briefly discuss the kinds of mistaken thinking identified by Ellis, Beck, and Martin Seligman (Abramson, Seligman, and Teasdale 1978). After that discussion I will help you understand what you can do to extricate yourself from these kinds of harmful automatic thoughts.

Ellis's Negative Beliefs

Albert Ellis identified a number of problematic negative beliefs that could contribute to your feeling needlessly miserable. He was quick to point out that negative beliefs, in and of themselves, are not a problem, but that you need to develop skills to dispute your negative beliefs when they are false.

The most noteworthy negative beliefs identified by Ellis (1962) are:

- *Awfulization.* This term refers to a tendency to see an incident or situation as awful, disastrous, horrible, etc.

- *Low frustration tolerance.* Ellis and his followers noted that difficulty accepting low levels of frustration are evidenced by frequent use of statements about things being "too hard," intolerable, or unbearable.

- *Global Rating.* Ellis refers here to the tendency to characterize yourself or others in an absolute (but negative) manner such as saying you are stupid, a loser, garbage, or worthless.

Ellis described four core beliefs that he felt

were the cornerstone of these types of negative thinking. One was the belief or expectation that you should be free of discomfort, in essence a demand that you should be able to be comfortable. Another was the expectation or demand that nearly everyone should love and approve of you, *just because*. This is similar to his "must" that others should treat you fairly and kindly, or if they do not, they "should" be condemned. A third core demand identified by Ellis was that you should be successful at the things you strive to do or find important. He also identified this as one of the three basic (problematic) "musts": "I must do well or I am no good." Finally, Ellis may have been the first to point out how toxic it can be to demand that things "should" or "should not" be a certain way, which he characterized as inflexible and dogmatic thinking.

Aaron Beck's Cognitive Distortions

Dr. Aaron Beck (1967) emphasized automatic cognitive (thinking-based) thoughts that were exaggerated or distorted in such a way that they made you more prone to feel depressed or anxious. These thoughts included beliefs, but also any thoughts that were distorted in a characteristically negative way. Beck's theories and observations led the way for a wave of effective cognitive behavioral therapies for depression, and soon thereafter for anxiety.

He and his peers such as self-help expert David Burns (2008) identified a long list of cognitive distortions (inaccurate perceptions of reality) that were associated with emotional problems, and when addressed often led to remarkable and lasting positive changes in these areas. Here is a list of the distortions Beck and his followers have identified:

1. *Dichotomous Thinking* (also described as "all or nothing thinking"). In this kind of thinking things are seen as either black or white, right or wrong, good or bad. There are not any shades of grey, and it usually is accompanied by characterizations like "always" and "never." This type of thinking is usually inaccurate to the extreme and leaves little room for learning, circumstance, or nuanced understanding. Perfectionists are especially inclined to think this way.

2. *Overgeneralization.* If you overgeneralize, you tend to jump to hasty conclusions based on one small clue or incident, or with too little evidence. If you know the parable of the blind man and the elephant, this serves as a good example of the mistake you make when you draw an inaccurate abstraction based on a narrow viewpoint. A blind man examining the tip of an elephant's tail may think he is

perceiving a brush, while another examining the leg may believe he is dealing with a pillar. Overgeneralizing occurs when there is too little evidence, and it can, of course, be most toxic when the generalization routinely paints a more negative picture than the evidence justifies.

3. *Jumping to Conclusions.* A similar problem to overgeneralization is the tendency to jump to conclusions (especially when the conclusions are negative and not necessarily warranted by the limited data). Two prominent versions of this are mindreading and fortune telling. In mind reading you will read a verbal or nonverbal cue or cues (or for that matter no evidence at all) as a negative appraisal, disposition, or intention, when you don't really know what the other person is thinking or feeling. Fortune tellers (when prone to predict negative outcomes) expect the

worst, often with little or no evidence to support their expectation.

4. *Labeling (and Mislabeling).* Related to overgeneralizing, but more pernicious, is a tendency to label or stereotype someone in a caricatured way, based on far too little information. You can label yourself as lazy or stupid because you are not getting the math homework done, but in reality it is more likely because you are anxious about it, depressed, or have a thyroid problem; or your neighbor becomes a "turd" because he forgot to mow your lawn when you asked him to do so. Mislabeling is when you are overly harsh in your evaluation based on rigid beliefs. (for example, you decide your neighbor is warmonger when she prefers a political candidate whom you dislike).

5. *Filtering.* With filtering you focus exclusively on one of a few small negative aspects of an event, and filter out most or

all of the positives. This also can refer to a well-known phenomenon called confirmation bias. In confirmation bias, we attend more fully to information that conforms to our beliefs. We do this because we are motivated to feel we are consistent.

6. *Stacking the Deck.* Similar to filtering, stacking occurs when you characterize an incident in such a way that it unfairly reflects whatever actually happened, in order for your (negative) belief to be bolstered (at the expense of any competing appraisals). In stacking you are distorting in a manner characterized in the social psychological literature as a self-fulfilling prophecy (Merton 1948), but in this case it is the appraisal that is changed to bolster the belief.

7. *Magnification and Minimization.* In this type of thinking you give greater weight than others would to a perceived weakness

or threat, and lesser weight than others would to a virtue or success. Catastrophizing, (making mountains out of molehills, already discussed in the chapter on Worries that Work) is a prime example of magnification.

8. *Disqualifying.* When you discount positive events or feedback you can expect that there will be fewer positives in your life. A compliment, for example, is not accepted as genuine but written off as flattery. The "A" you received on the test was only because the test (or class) was too easy, it was not because you knew the subject matter that well. The positive performance appraisal at work is a reflection on the boss, who never noticed how badly you were doing.

9. *Should statements.* When you expect yourself—or others—to always behave in a certain way, when any reasonable person would cut them (or you) some slack, then

should statements are your problem. Due to a moral or ethical imperative, often rather arbitrary, you override more realistic evaluations and expectations because you "should" have done it better or differently. This was also noted above as one of Albert Ellis's distorted beliefs.

10. *Emotional Reasoning.* Making choices and evaluations based on feelings, rather than other variables. When you are depressed or anxious it is hard to ignore that strong feeling. However, just because the feeling is prominent doesn't mean it is an imperative. If you feel scared to leave the house, that does not mean that you are actually in such danger that you should not drive to work, or for that matter to get groceries. That, of course, would not apply if you are actually likely to have potential harm.

11. *Heaven's Reward.* If you believe this protestant work ethic rule (the same one

that Calvinism embraces), you are suffering for Heaven's Reward. With this kind of thinking you believe that hard work will get you into heaven (or a promotion for which you might otherwise barely qualify). Given this type of belief, you can easily end up expecting a spouse, boss, or roommate to appreciate your efforts more than they might be inclined. Just because you believe that vacuuming at least once a day is essential and virtuous, the roommate may, instead, find it annoying, especially at 8:00 a.m.

12. *Personalization.* This thinking involves situations wherein you blame yourself (or others) for things over which you actually have little or no control. Often a fallacy for parents, who think it is their fault when a child's grades are problematic or the child is arrested for fighting, when of course other factors are more likely to be at play.

13. *Blaming.* Less of a factor in anxiety or depression, the fallacy of blaming others when they have no control does nevertheless adds a certain level of misery to your life, because you are less likely to engage in any self-improvement if a negative outcome is always due to the other person's shortcomings.

14. *Fallacy of Change.* If you can just get him/her to change, then everything will be ok. Really? How likely is that? You are more likely to be able to change yourself (including this belief), than the other person. The other person may not want to change, or see the pressing need for change that you see.

Attributional Errors

Martin Seligman and his colleagues at the University of Pennsylvania also have identified some characteristic thinking errors in their attempt to explain learned helplessness. Learned helplessness is a central phenomenon in depression that occurs when your payoffs and punishments seem to be random at best, and unconnected to your efforts. You begin to believe that nothing you do will matter. In their attributional reformulation of learned helplessness, Seligman and colleagues emphasized the role of causal attributions, especially in depression. When you explain events in your life that are ambiguous, the kinds of explanations you routinely make can impact your mood, when the explanations are made in a (negatively) biased way.

Depressed and anxious patients seem to characteristically explain a murky situation in ways that predispose them to feel helplessness, hopelessness, and dread. In this model, three dimensions of causal explanations were found to be especially relevant to mood disorders.

Depressed individuals tend to be overly prone

to assign negative events to their own culpability and positive events to things outside themselves. For anxiety, your explanations for positive events apparently are less of a factor, but, if you are anxious, you do show a characteristic bias with negative events in which you would tend to blame yourself more often than others.

A second dimension that the attributional model of learned helplessness notes as problematic is the tendency of depressed persons to see negative events as chronic and long lasting, while positive events are dismissed as brief and transient. For anxiety again it is the negative events that are the typical problem, and you will tend to be overly prone to describe negative events as long lasting and persistent.

The third dimension for which depressed patients demonstrate a biased attributional style has to do with specificity. Positive outcomes can be more easily ignored if they are seen as only occurring in the situation at hand, whereas negative results are generalized to all or most situations. For anxious patients, your negative outcome is typically seen as more universally applied to most situations (this bias is probably less true if you have a phobia). Again, positive outcomes appear to be less a factor for anxiety than depression.

So, what can you do about these thoughts?

If you have more than your fair share of anxiety and/or depression you probably recognized several of the beliefs, thoughts and attributions above, as "just the way I think." Even if you recognized that these thoughts play a significant role in your emotional problems, you may not believe you can change these thoughts. After all, you are likely to say, "I have thought that way all my life, and I can't change now," or "You can't teach an old dog new tricks."

Really? People can't learn? Wisdom is only possible in youth? Logic would show you that the very statement that you are using to rationalize not changing, (being no longer able to change) is on its face, at least a very bad distortion, and I am here to tell you that it will contribute to your problems if you cling to it.

While youth under 25 have a brain that is still growing, learning doesn't stop after that. The brain retains plasticity (is neurologically adaptive) and new neural pathways are laid down every day, often specifically aimed at consolidating your new learning. So beliefs and thoughts that seemed useful when you were young, fortunately are not fixed, and can be updated. What about the roles of wisdom and experience? Isn't it possible that you understand, for example, ridicule or bullying better now than when you were in middle school?

And what about old dogs? I recently taught my 14+ year old dachshund to wink. That's like a 98 year old senior citizen, translated from dog years.

These negative thoughts that you have been having, the ones that Aaron Beck, Albert Ellis, and Martin Seligman contend are at least as big a factor in your moods as your genes—these thoughts are typically just over-learned habits. They may have been the best explanation you could come up with in the lunch room in sixth grade, but by now that way of thinking is just an unexamined old habit. Bad habits can be broken. We know how. You already know how, because you have changed before: practice.

How do we learn a new skill? If it is a brand new skill, we can rely on the plasticity of the brain. It takes repetition to learn something new, and you actually continually build new neural brain circuits when you learn. Whether learning to play Texas Holdem or to think more effectively, you can build new brain pathways that lead to new (and improved) thinking habits.

These new learnings can replace the old habits: the negative thoughts.

Cognitive behavioral therapists are, at a basic level, asking you to change your brain wiring by learning something new. Experts vary on how many repetitions they believe are needed to learn something new. Some say as few as seven, and old wives tales say as many as 33 repetitions. The number is likely in between; I tell my patients a good number is about 18, if you want to have confidence that you have developed a new habit.

However, other factors besides repetition can effect this "new" learning. If the learning is nonsense material, it takes more repetitions, while if it is meaningful it is easier to remember, requiring fewer repetitions. Research also shows that "spaced" practice is better than a concentrated, day after day, repetition. Practice on Monday and Tuesday then take two days off, and then maybe four days in a row, then another break, that sort of thing.

In most cases in CBT, we are not only learning a new habit (a new, more accurate thought), but we are also getting rid of (extinguishing) an older competing habit (the automatic negative thought that is the culprit). The good news is there is some good evidence that learning a new habit is helpful in breaking an old one, so it is faster to have an improved, healthier replacement thought at the ready.

So, you have a negative, old habitual thought that pops into your head often when things go poorly. Maybe you think you are a loser, or that you *always* make bad decisions. I may be able to convince you that thinking that way stacks the deck against you, so things will assuredly go even more badly, but how can you change that? The following are some useful steps you can take to help guide you through the process.

Step One

The first step is to identify the negative thoughts that you want to change. Often it is helpful to carry around a notepad, or use a cellphone app like Evernote, and jot down all the thoughts that sound even a little negative, no matter how familiar and true they initially feel. Do this for at least a week or two.

Step Two

If you have a therapist then you and your psychologist could go over these thoughts and pick out 20 or so that are both frequent and not usually in your best interest. If you do not have a therapist, the negative thoughts and beliefs listed earlier in this chapter might give you some guidance. Examine your list of negative thoughts to see if they are thoughts that Beck, Ellis and others have identified as harmful. Many of these negative thoughts do not hold up very well to close scrutiny. For example, it may seem real when you tell yourself that you always make bad decisions, but the fact that you chose to read this book proves you can and do sometimes make good decisions.

You likely will have an almost sentimental attachment to some of the old dysfunctional thought patterns, but while that thought or belief may be true *sometimes*, more likely than not these negative thoughts are way overused, or applied to too many situations where they just don't square up. Again, a therapist will have more experience with identifying these types of errors.

Remember, just because a thought pops into your head does not mean it is true. It might have been useful or even true at one time, but now you can think with greater wisdom and experience, compared to when you first established these lines of thought. Look at enough of them to start to get a sense for what is irrational and unduly negative.

Step 3

You do not have to deal with all these automatic thoughts and completely remake yourself. In fact, it is best to pick just a few of the 20 for now, targeting some of your more frequently deployed negative thoughts. Pick thoughts that you can clearly recognize as bad habits, but not the thoughts to which you cling most strongly. You want to start with something easier. It is helpful to get some success under your belt before taking on the more strongly held (but still inaccurate) thoughts and beliefs. The three or four thoughts you select I will refer to as your targets.

Now for these targets, I want you to look closely at them and figure out why they may not be true. Often they are a little true but way overstated or too broadly applied. What is the essence of the thought, and how can you restate it in a manner that is more accurate, less negative, and more consistent with an adult or logical view of the world? For example, if you typically think "I always make bad decisions," a more positive alternative might be the thought that "I need to read a book on decision making," or "I need to start being less impulsive when I make decisions." The new thought should be true, practical, and resonant with who you are.

Step 4a: Fact Checking (traditional CBT)

Now, if we are using CBT, we are going to start making some changes in your brain. You are going to use two types of skills to take on these target negative thoughts. One skill is learning to fact check, and the other is called thought stopping.

With fact checking, every time you notice a target thought, you check to see if it is a fact or an opinion. You dispute the thought, holding it up to the light of logic and reason. If your negative thought is something like "I know she thinks I am lazy because I didn't do (insert household task here) but I just can't do it, at least not feeling this tired." Here are some things you might dispute:

1. You do not know what she is thinking, you are assuming (mindreading). Do you really know her mind? She may be thinking about what to make for dinner tonight, or the vacation plans she wants to discuss with you, or a bill she has to pay, or contemplating if you might be depressed. She might be even wondering if you care at all about what she thinks or feels (while you of course are assuming you already know). Simply put, if you don't know what she is thinking, your guess is likely as not to be rather off the mark. Don't be a mind reader.

2. OK, so let's say you somehow read her mind (guessed right) and she is thinking of

you, and your immediate interaction. She might feel pleased that you are being quiet, for once. She can get a break from your nagging.

3. If she is thinking about you, what makes you so sure it is a negative appraisal (other than that is always what you tend to think)? Now let's say (and at this point I don't put much stock in your assumptions because your negative bias is showing) that you are a great mind reader, and you are almost certain from the scowl on her face that it is not a positive thought she is having. Even then you don't know *what* she is thinking. Maybe she thinks you don't find her attractive any more, since it has been so long since you had sex. Or maybe she hates that striped shirt you always seem to like, or the TV show you are watching. Or perhaps she is concerned because you did not remember you were supposed to pick up the dry cleaning.

4. How about the phrase "I can't do it!" Maybe if you did a little of that task you would feel better. Baby steps often help get a project going, and you might actually find yourself feeling less tired.

You get the idea. Start holding your target thoughts up for inspection. For fact checking to work best you need to change it and make it yours. I think the idea of fact checking suits a newspaper reporter well, while if you are a lawyer you might instead cross-examine the thoughts. If you like logic, attack it with logic. If you have a great sense of humor, then make fun out of it. Find a method that suits you and go after that target thought, make it justify itself as true and not just an opinion.

The idea behind fact checking is to disrupt the thought. Once you have begun to successfully examine the negative target thought, you can start adding in the alternative thought you already prepared, or even better, come up with a new alternative belief or thought right there in the moment. A practical note: it often helps to write the thought down, right away during the phase, and dispute it in writing as well, so you don't have to do it all in your head. It also can help to use some self-talk, addressing yourself by your own name and taking yourself to task for that negative thinking.

Thought Stopping

Some thoughts are especially hard to rid yourself of, and a technique with more oomph may be needed. This is especially true for thoughts that are fear-based or urges related to addictions. These may well be conditioned responses that can seem very compelling, and persistently vexing. Examples include phobias, obsessions and compulsions, and urges and thoughts that sustain addictive behaviors. Before you can argue against (reality check) one of these types of thoughts, you may need to put some extra effort into interrupting them, at least when they persist. (A note of caution here. Exposure and extinction might be a better choice for these kinds of thoughts, and becoming obsessed with fighting them can make it worse, and not better.)

If you are approaching this entirely from the vantage of interrupting your most persistent negative thoughts, you might choose to use *Thought Stopping* to bolster your success. This method was developed by Wolpe (1966) as a treatment for obsessive ruminations. It was later refined by other clinicians, who applied it to problems ranging from heroin addiction urges to depression.

In Thought Stopping CBT, you would sit quietly in a chair with your therapist, with your eyes closed. When the target thought or urge emerges, you signal with a finger, and the therapist startles you with a loud "STOP" while you are supposed to envision a stop sign or the word "stop." The loud "stop" should be sufficiently impactful to produce a startle response. In using it to treat heroin addiction urges, clinicians might have you imagine a swarm of bees or wasps coming at you.

In the self-help version of the same technique, you clear your mind and when the thought arises, you picture the stop sign and yell (inside your head) the word "stop" with emphatic vigor.

For this technique to be helpful, you need to make a few modifications. For one thing, you do not want to use this in the earliest stages, because at that point your task is primarily to become aware of and recognize the problem thoughts. With *Thought Stopping* you want to be stopping the thought itself and not your introspection that notices the negative thought. If *Thought Stopping* works, it is guided by the behavioral principal that what *immediately* precedes the startle is reduced because of the instant introduction of the punishing consequence. You are best served when you employ a technique like *Thought Stopping* when the thought still persists, even after you have caught it, (e.g., a sticky thought) and are trying to interrupt it.

The other main concern is that you want to be sure to have handy your already prepared counter-thought. As soon as you stop or interrupt the old thought, immediately bring forth the new, more positive thought. The idea is to interrupt the negative thought, and then in its absence replace it with the new thought.

Problems with *Thought Stopping*

Several misapplications of *thought stopping* have caused it to fall into disfavor, and you should avoid using it at all if you are going to make these mistakes.

Many popular psychologists and internet anxiety "experts" have suggested that to get rid of an unwanted thought you can wear a rubber band around your wrist, and when you have the target thought you snap hard on the rubber band to "punish" it. Those who advocate this technique are even prone to calling it *thought stopping*, but it is not an effective tool when applied that way.

Two problems with this technique are evident. First, as already discussed above, when you snap the rubber band after first noticing the negative thought, you are punishing not the thought itself but the act of noticing it. If you were devising rewards and punishments for thoughts you would want to reward and not punish self-awareness, especially in the early stages of treatment. What you would want to punish, if anything, would be the persistence of the thoughts in the face of a new better thought. The other problem with the rubber band version of *thought stopping* is that punishment is notoriously bad at generalizing to other situations. Behavioral psychologists will prefer rewards over punishment almost every time, as you get much more effective learning when it is applied more generally.

Wegner (1989) in an early study, found that attempts to suppress a thought just make it stronger. If you want to banish a thought you will have better luck if you restructure it. Make fun of it. Analyze it. Treat it like an unwelcome guest or a heckler, and then replace it with a better thought.

In the end, thought stopping could be a useful adjunct to your CBT, but only if you apply it wisely. It should be used primarily on fear- or anger-based persistent thoughts, phobias, and urges. If you are successful in interrupting (not banishing) the thought, then replace or modify the thought with a new more realistic or helpful thought.

Step 4b: A Mindfulness Version of CBT

If you are inclined to use mindfulness or meditation, a less combative and more accepting stance is available to you at this point when dealing with negative target thoughts. Instead of reality checks, thought stopping, or logical dissection and restructuring of the thought, Mindfulness CBT is more likely to emphasize awareness and curiosity about these thoughts.

Approaching negative thoughts mindfully, you notice them but do not give them much attention, and you avoid actually battling them. You shift back attention to your senses, or your breathing, or whatever you set out to focus on, making note of the fact that you had a negative thought. The negative thought itself (or at least the affect connected to it) would tend to lose its charge, when not given great weight; this is essentially an exposure paradigm. You can notice that the thought occurred or note with curiosity a specific cognitive error you made, but with mindfulness you do not dispute the thought, but simply make note of it. When you are done with a mindfulness session in which you noticed some negative thinking, you might also take other practical steps to address the depression, anxiety or stress, now that you have noticed it.

Step Five: Going Wide

Once you have had some success with your target thoughts, take the same approach and start to address all the 20 or so thoughts you initially identified. As you begin to master those, look for others that also need to be revised and updated.

Chapter Six

All in Your Head? Physiological Factors in Anxiety, Stress and Panic

You can skip this final chapter if you find biology and psychophysiology boring, or already have a good understanding of the brain and body connections related to anxiety. I do not aspire here to go into great depth, and most of the concepts I cover here, such as fight or flight responses, are probably already familiar to you from an introductory psychology class in college. However, I have found that for my patients, laying it out the way I do in this final chapter will help you make sense out of that information and puts it in a more personal context.

Fight or Flight

If you are accustomed to thinking of anxiety as a disorder or lifelong illness it can be helpful for you to understand that much of what you are calling anxiety is not only a natural and normal process, but a healthy process when managed properly. The physical processes, when understood correctly, are a systematic and finely tuned set of balanced internal regulations that can be harnessed to your benefit.

While the stress and strife of everyday living impacts everyone, you may not realize the extent to which your body can become accustomed to staying keyed up and wound tightly. If you are anxious, you likely stay tense and ready to deal with any threatening adversaries, real or anticipated.

Walter B. Cannon (1915), a Harvard Physiologist, first identified the physical components of the human reaction to perceived danger, and called it the "Fight or Flight Response." Later, Hans Selye (1976), in his explanation of stress, considered this fight or flight response to be the first stage of a three-stage stress response he termed the General Adaptation Syndrome.

The acute physical reaction when you are stressed or endangered seems to be hardwired into your genes and body. When I ask my clients how they know they are anxious, they often point to this set of physiological reactions (e.g., rapid heartbeat, muscle tension). While these physical changes are often considered anxiety, and even seen by medicine as an illness, these functional changes have an origin in the reactions—adaptive and helpful—that have ensured your survival in the face of danger.

When you detect that you have an adversary, your body and brain automatically make several changes, in order to help you deal with the perceived threat. Without these changes you wouldn't be very likely to survive.

If you were concerned that a saber-tooth tiger may be outside your door, it wouldn't be surprising for your body to make a few rapid changes. It would probably be helpful, in that case, if some of your bigger muscles tensed, so that you could run away and seek safety, or stay and fight the tiger if you thought you could win. You might think that anxiety would be less physiologically reactive than fear, but you would be mistaken. Anxiety is really closer to fear squared. If you are afraid of a tiger, you at least know what to do: run! But what if you are not sure if it's a tiger or a Doberman Pincer? And whose Doberman is it? Should you try to pet it? But it sure looks like a tiger, and it has really big teeth. The added uncertainty compounds the fear, and your body works overtime to gear you up.

In addition to muscle tension, you would probably be better off if you had some extra oxygen as fuel. That is why, in times of stress or danger, you often breathe short rapid shallow breaths, without consciously choosing to do so, to assure you have plenty of oxygen. Your body also pumps stress hormones like cortisol and adrenaline at the first signs of threat. Adrenaline tends to last about 15 minutes, and cortisol is responsible for extending the effect for a longer interval.

Your body also makes several other changes. For example, the last thing you need to do when you're running away from (or fighting) the tiger, is to digest your food. Indeed Cannon's first relevant discovery—the one that put him on the trail of Fight or Flight—was that when you are afraid, your digestive system shuts off your peristaltic digestive waves. You also stop secreting saliva and most other digestive juices, hence the dry mouth you experience when you are anxious.

It seems we are not designed to be eating while running, McDonald's and other fast food establishments notwithstanding. Rather, we are designed to be eating while sitting around the campfire telling stories about how we got away. Anything in your stomach, during your fight or flight predicament, just sits there. When it starts up again, there has been a lump sitting in your stomach and the digestive system is thrown off. It is not surprising that diarrhea, gas, and other stomach symptoms often occur when you are dealing with anxiety and stress.

Another change in your body during fight or flight is that the blood in your system is diverted away from the smaller veins and vessels and is directed instead to the core of your body (the axis between your heart and the back of your head) and to your larger muscles. The blood drains away from your skin and your extremities, such as your hands and feet, can become cold and clammy as a result. If you noticed that your hands shake or you find yourself tapping your feet, anxiously, you may have described this as nerves. But the shaky hands is really an involuntary shiver, and you probably learned as early as childhood to wring your hands and fidget in a manner that would warm your hands at least a little at those times.

Your body may be smarter than you realize, because if that tiger took a bite out of your leg or hand, or you stepped on a sharp rock, you would not bleed out. In fact, if I were to come across an accident I could tell you whether or not the driver saw it coming. If there was a lot of blood for an equivalent injury, there would be a good chance that the driver was blindsided and had no time to react. Because there was no time to pull the blood in to the center of the body, away from the injuries, there was more bleeding.

These and other reactions, like high blood pressure, rapid heartbeat, and dilated eyes are all part of the network of physiological reactions to fear and stress. The systems described above are coordinated and intricately balanced mechanisms geared towards survival. They are part of a neurological system called the autonomic nervous system, and the accompanying neuro-hormonal system.

Physiological Anxiety is a reaction to threat, but it is often a threat that you are not consciously able to identify. In modern society, there aren't as many saber-tooth tigers, but the cost—especially in the western civilization—is that we walk around in a constant state of readiness to run from that tiger, or boss, but with no place to run.

Your body reacts more or less automatically, and this physical readiness is handled by the autonomic nervous system. The part of autonomic system that keeps you "raring to go" is referred to as the sympathetic nervous system (think of it as sympathetic to your task of getting to safety). What many people don't realize is that there is also a parallel system, known as the parasympathetic nervous system, which is designed to reverse that extra energy and move towards a more relaxed state.

Your body is a cleverly crafted system of checks and balances, and the parasympathetic nervous system involves all the mirror image (opposite) reactions than are noted in fight or flight responses, but they are now geared instead to calming down, or relaxing that system. Instead of rapid short breaths, you can take deep full breaths at a slow and relaxing pace. We can relax the muscles, and we can find methods to warm our hands and feet, to make them warm and toasty.

All of these relaxing responses are normally mobilized in an unconscious manner, automatically, just like the sympathetic nervous system, which is also often out of your awareness. However, most of us are not nearly as good at switching to a needed lower gear, however skilled we are at getting "keyed up." Many of the stress management techniques and other skills that psychologists teach, like the breathing techniques covered in Chapter Two, are aimed directly at mobilizing the part of our nervous system that is geared to relaxing.

Understanding the role your body plays in anxiety and stress, and knowing about the Fight or Flight Response, can be an important first step in learning to effectively manage your anxiety and signs of stress. Whether done as part of psychotherapy, or as a self-help effort, learning to relax is a skill that can pay health dividends.

Amygdala- The Seat of Emotions

The amygdala plays an important role in the brain's relationship to feelings, especially to fear, anger, and anxiety. It is a small almond-shaped area in the medial temporal lobe of the brain (behind your ear). This bundle of connected nuclei that is part of the limbic system is sometimes referred to as the seat of emotions.

The amygdala seems to play a role in anxiety and in the conditioning reaction to fear. PTSD-related memories are likely at least partly processed in the amygdala itself, as are other conditioned learning events.

Another way the amygdala is involved in anxiety is that, together with the hippocampus (a nearby brain structure), it influences what fear- and anxiety-related memories are laid down and where in the brain they are stored. If your brain is considered trainable, one of the areas that needs new memories and learning are the fear-conditioned reactions processed by the amygdala.

Panic Attacks, Severe Anxiety, and Hyperventilation

In a panic attack—seemingly out of the blue—your body feels like it has gone totally out of control. A sense of suffocation, chest pain, trembling, and flushed skin, all combine with a host of other symptoms to make you feel like you are having a heart attack, are going to die, or are losing control.

Persons who experience a panic attack are noted to have many of these symptoms:

- a sensation of suffocation or smothering;
- a rapid heartbeat, chest tightness, or pain;
- anxiety or fear over losing control or going crazy;
- dizziness and fainting;
- shortness of breath;
- numbness or tingling sensations;
- profuse sweating;
- cold, clammy hands, feet, or both;
- nausea or stomach ache;
- a strong need to move, and to avoid feeling trapped.

What are all these symptoms, and how do they cascade out of control so that you can completely—if temporarily—seem to lose it?

Some panic attacks seem to come from nowhere, however these "out of the blue" panic attacks are most often are part of a flashback, triggered by a cue that reminds you of a past threat, one about which you may not be at all conscious. These flashbacks are beyond the scope of the current book.

Many panic attacks, however, build gradually as a part of day from an ongoing anxious lifestyle. If you tend to be anxious and walk around with a great deal of stress and apprehension, then you will begin to experience an escalation of the aforementioned symptoms that are a part of the sympathetic nervous system. If you fail to counter the revved-up state with techniques like deep breathing or other grounding techniques, then the problem will likely continue to build. You might be so used to high levels of stress that you do not even know it, but soon your muscles are tight, your hands are cold, your heart is beating rapidly, and you are taking rapid shallow breaths much like a pant. If you are breathing rapidly but not spending oxygen in a rapid escape, the store of extra oxygen begins to build up in your system.

In panic attacks the oxygen is the problem, combined with a mistaken reaction your mind makes that aggravates your dilemma. To understand the type of error in understanding that leads to a panic attack, I want to detour briefly to a similar mistake we often make. Only this one has to do with hunger.

There are several "thermostat-like" switches in your body that regulate your physiological processes, and one such switch is what we often mistakenly call hunger. Humans are notoriously poor at reporting whether we are hungry. In stomach operations when the surgeon needs to inflate a balloon in the stomach, to assist in surgical maneuvers, people cannot reliably report a sense of fullness versus emptiness when the balloon is inflated or deflated. Similarly, most

Type II diabetics, despite measuring blood glucose several times a day with a pin prick and gauge that reports sugar levels, are not good reporters either. They have poor accuracy in predicting the level of glucose. The really skilled Type II diabetics can tell when something is wrong, but there is much less ability to tell whether the glucose level is too high or too low.

Yet we all think we can recognize hunger, correct? What we think is hunger is often actually thirst. You know the signal, the morning after a hangover that says, "OMG let's get some water now!" That's the signal I am talking about. Only we think it is hunger most of the time, so we eat. And most food has enough water in it, compared to our bodies, so that when we eat enough we eventually satisfy our thirst. This is a very inefficient mistake that we think we are hungry, and fix the thirst by eating, which leads eventually to quenching it, but with a side effect of way too much weight gain.

That is why most diets tell you to drink a lot of water. They simplify it by saying that "water fills you up," but they don't go into the details I just did, about why and how. Water quenches your "hunger."

We make a similar mistake in panic attacks. In panic, it is all about the balance between the oxygen and carbon dioxide. Just like the trees we need both oxygen and carbon dioxide, but while the trees need a lot more carbon dioxide, we need a lot more oxygen; we need both to function in a healthy and well manner. There is another switch inside our brain that keeps track of that balance; how much oxygen and carbon dioxide we have in relationship to each other. There is an optimal balance and the "thermostat" is quiet when we have the approximately correct ratio. However when the ratio goes too far off—when it detects an imbalance, then the sensor tells us something is wrong. It does not tell us that there is too much or too little of either, but that one is too high compared to the other.

Now most of our experience with that switch going off occurs when you are not getting enough oxygen (compared to the carbon dioxide). When you try to show off how long you can hold your breath underwater that is when you get that signal, and it sends you scurrying to the top of the pool to get some more air. Or when the ragweed and pollen coats your car with yellow stuff, it can be hard to breathe, and you feel you might suffocate, that's another time you feel it. So most of the time when you feel that signal, it seems to mean you need oxygen.

But if you are anxious already and have started to do a lot of rapid shallow breathing, and you are not running away from the tiger, then the imbalance you are feeling is not too little oxygen, but too much. But since you mistakenly believe (because of the signal) that you are suffocating, you breathe more, which does not fix the problem. The "cure" makes it worse, and you feel you are suffocating even more. So you breathe more, which makes it even worse. It spirals out of control into hyperventilation and a panic attack, if allowed to progress.

If you went to an emergency room, with a panic attack (you probably thought it was a heart attack), then in the olden days they would have you breathe into and out of a brown paper bag. Much to your surprise that worked (as you were breathing in mostly carbon dioxide and with that, the ratio of carbon dioxide to oxygen soon returns to normal). Of course without Nurse Ratchett standing over you, it is not easy to do the paper bag trick on your own.

Fortunately the breathing exercises discussed in Chapter Two do the trick nicely, without the paper bag. Because you are breathing deeply you are not concerned that you will suffocate. However, the way you learned these techniques, if you followed the instructions, there will gradually be less oxygen than carbon dioxide (you spend less time breathing in) and the carbon dioxide begins to return to normal, as you do the breathing technique. That is why you want to learn to breathe in that type of manner, not just to turn on the parasympathetic relaxation response but to help ward off (or more quickly turn around) the carbon dioxide/oxygen problem that leads to panic and hyperventilation.

Conclusion

Thank you for the opportunity to share with you some of the approaches that I have found helpful in my clinical practice, when I was helping my clients deal with anxiety-related problems. These ideas and techniques were only a small portion of what I utilize, but I tried to describe the ones I use most frequently and across many kinds of anxiety. I certainly did not invent them all. If I have explained them in a manner that has been helpful, I hope you will credit my patients as well as my mentors, all of whom have helped me to understand and explain it more clearly over the years, and to develop and refine the tools so they work better.

I hope to discuss some special topics related to anxiety in my next book in this series, including social anxiety, hair pulling and skin picking, body image disorders, phobias, and obsessive compulsive problems. Some of these problems can be addressed in part with the techniques outlined in this book, but more specialized techniques are often called for when dealing with these special issues.

The Usual Disclaimers

While this book is offered as information and education, you might be able to make use of some of these ideas as one component of your efforts to help yourself. This information is in no way intended as a substitute for therapy, medical care, or the excellent attention a psychologist would give you, should you seek the individualized assistance of a therapist. I make no warranty for the effectiveness of these techniques for any individual. Good therapy takes into account many factors before devising an intervention, and this book is not in and of itself sufficient. Indeed these ideas do not go beyond generic advice because your individual and unique situation is known only to you.

If you have your own therapist, he or she will, in consultation with you, be able to tailor the kinds of interventions outlined to your very specific needs, talents, and circumstances. This book does not replace the rewarding and hard work of therapy done with a professional, nor can it replace the self-discovery that you can do on your own, by reading several books like this, integrating that knowledge, applying it, and most especially by exploring within to find your own resources and solutions.

If you found *Overcoming Anxiety* to be helpful consider joining Dr. Berndt's Psychology Knowledge Readers Group where, as a charter member, you can get free excerpts and other useful information, as well as keep track of new materials as they come available. Join at http://psychologyknowledge.com

About the Author

David Berndt, Ph.D. is a licensed clinical psychologist and author, who currently lives in beautiful Charleston, SC. where he has a private practice downtown near the College of Charleston. His doctorate in clinical psychology is from Loyola University, and he published or presented more than 80 papers when he was at the University of Chicago, where he attained the rank of Associate Clinical Professor of Psychiatry. Dr. Berndt is best known as the author of the adult and children's versions of the *Multiscore Depression Inventory*, published by Western Psychological Services. Dr. Berndt also contributes to several websites and blogs, including http://psychologyknoweldge.com.

Appendix - References

Abramson, Lyn Y., Martin E. P. Seligman, and John D. Teasdale. 1978. "Learned helplessness in humans: Critique and reformulation." *Journal of Abnormal Psychology*. 87, 49-74.

Bandler, Richard and John Grinder. 1979. *Frogs into Princes: Neuro Linguistic Programming*. Boulder, Co: Real People Press.

Bandler, John, and Richard Grinder. 1981. *Trance-Formations Neuro-Linguistic Programming and the Structure of Hypnosis,* Boulder, Co: Real People Press.

Beck, Aaron T. 1967. *The diagnosis and management of depression.* Philadelphia: University of Pennsylvania Press.

Burns, David. 2008. *Feeling Good: The New Mood Therapy*, New York: Harper.

Cannon, Walter B. 1915. *Bodily Changes in Pain, Hunger Fear and Rage*. New York: Appleton & Company.

Dolan, Yvonne. 1991. *Resolving Sexual Abuse: Solution-focused therapy and Ericksonian Hypnosis for Survivors*. New York: Norton Publishing.

Dolan, Yvonne. 2000. *One Small Step, Moving Beyond Trauma and Therapy to a Life of Joy.* Ontario, Canada: Author's Choice Press.

Ellis, Albert. 1962. *Reason and Emotion in Psychotherapy*. New York: Stuart

Greenson, Jeffrey M. 2008. "Mindfulness Research Update 2008" *Complementary Health Practice Review* 14(1): 10-18

Hofmann, Stefan G., Alice T. Sawyer, Ashley A. Witt, and Diana Oh. 2010. "The effect of mindfulness-based therapy on Anxiety and Depression; A meta-analytic review." *Journal of Consulting and Clinical Psychology.* 78 (10): 169-183.

Jones, Moran D. 1998. *The Thinker's Toolkit: 14 Powerful Techniques for Problem Solving.* New York: Crown.

Kabat-Zinn, Jon. 1990. *Full Catastrophe Living: Using the Wisdom of Your Body and Mind to Face Stress, Pain, and Illness.* New York: Dell.

Kabat-Zinn, Jon. 2003. "Mindfulness-based interventions in context: Past, present, and future." *Clinical Psychology, Science and Practice*, 10(2): 144-156.

Merton, Robert K. 1968. *Social Theory and Social Structure*. New York: Free Press.

Rodriguez, Christina M. and Phillipa Pehi. 1998. *Depression, Anxiety and Attributional Style.* New Zealand Journal of Psychology: 27 (1).

Rosen, Sidney. 1991 *My Voice Will Go With You, the Teaching Tales of Milton Erickson,* New York: Norton

Sears, Richard W., Tirch, D. & Denton, R. 2011. *Mindfulness in Clinical Practice.* Sarasota, FL : Professional Resource Press.

Selye, Hans. 1976. *Stress in health and disease.* Reading, MA: Butterworth.

Shapiro, Francine. 2001. *Eye Movement Desensitization and Reprocessing (EMDR): Basic Principles, Protocols, and Procedures, 2nd Edition.* New York: Guilford.

Stampfl, T. G., and Lewis, D. J. 1967. "Essentials of implosive therapy: A learning-theory-based psychodynamic behavioral therapy." *Journal of Abnormal Psychology*, 72, 496-503.

Stracker, David. 1997. *Rapid Problem Solving with Post-It Notes.* Boston: DaCapo.

Wegner, Daniel M. 1989. *White bears and other unwanted thoughts: Suppression, obsession, and the psychology of mental control.* New York: Penguin.

Wolpe, Joseph. 1958. *Psychotherapy by reciprocal Inhibition*. Stanford, CA: Stanford University Press.

CPSIA information can be obtained
at www.ICGtesting.com
Printed in the USA
LVHW081149020419
612663LV00033B/761/P

9 781514 327241